koreastyle

WITHDRAWN

Marcia Iwatate and Kim Unsoo

Introduction by Clark E. Llewellyn
Photographs by Lee Jongkeun

TUTTLE PUBLISHING
Tokyo • Rutland, Vermont • Singapore

Published by Tuttle Publishing, an imprint of Periplus
Editions (HK) Ltd, with editorial offices at 364 Innovation
Drive, North Clarendon, Vermont 05759, USA, and 130
Joo Seng Road #06-01, Singapore 368357.

Text and photographs © 2006 Periplus Editions (Hong Kong) Ltd

Library of Congress Control Number 2005910956
ISBN 10 0 8048 3750 3
ISBN 13 978 0 8048 3750 7

Authors' Note: Three romanization systems are commonly
used for the Korean Hangul script: Revised Romanization of
Korean (officially adopted by the government since 2000),
McCune-Reischauer (most commonly used until 2000), and
Yale Romanization (mainly used in linguistics). As a result,
many inconsistencies prevail. For example, the period name
Joseon frequently referred to in this book is also spelt
Choson, Chosun, and Joson. We have employed the Revised
Romanization of Korean for the texts except in personal
names, out of respect for the individuals, and for words
that are already familiar in the English language in the old
spelling, such as *kimchi* and *ginseng*. Readers may refer to
the following for details:
http://en.wikipedia.org/wiki/Revised_Romanization_of_Korean
We have also adopted the Korean and Japanese way of
presenting names, with the family name first.

Distributed by:

North America, Latin America and Europe
Tuttle Publishing, 364 Innovation Drive, North Clarendon,
Vermont 05759, USA.
Tel: (802) 773 8930; Fax: (802) 773 6993
info@tuttlepublishing.com
www.tuttlepublishing.com

Japan
Tuttle Publishing, Yaekari Building, 3F, 5-4-12 Osaki,
Shinagawa-ku, Tokyo 141-0032.
Tel: (813) 5437 0171; Fax: (813) 5437 0755
tuttle-sales@gol.com

Asia Pacific
Berkeley Books Pte Ltd, 130 Joo Seng Road #06-01/03,
Singapore 368357.
Tel: (65) 6280 1330; Fax: (65) 6280 6290
inquiries@periplus.com.sg
www.periplus.com

10 09 08 07 06
8 7 6 5 4 3 2 1

Printed in Singapore

Endpapers: Lock Museum and Residence (page 28)
Page 1: Glass House (page 60)
Page 2: Reincarnation of a Bygone Era (page 190)
Pages 4–5: Hanok Case Study (page 138)
Pages 6–7: Square within a Square (page 212)

contents

8   **Korean Aesthetics, Modern Directions**

18   Metropolitan Sanctuary
28   Lock Museum and Residence
40   Historical Stone Wall House
50   Fashion Designer's Muse
60   Glass House
68   Treasure Trove
78   Poetry of Wire
86   Mountain Atelier
92   Traditional Couturier's Salon
100   House of Voids
108   Camerata Music Studio and Residence
116   Folding Screen Mountain Retreat
128   Living with Art
138   Hanok Case Study
146   Reflex Penthouse
152   Collector's Hillside Haven
160   Photographer's Hideaway
166   Bedrock Manor
174   Maestro's Utopian Vision
182   Tribute to Korean Modernism
190   Reincarnation of a Bygone Era
196   Showcase of Art
204   Masterpiece of Confucian Architecture
212   Square within a Square

224   Credits

korean aesthetics, modern directions

CLARK E. LLEWELLYN

KOREA STYLE is epitomized by the beauty and humility observed in the offering of a cup of tea with two hands gently folded while lightly grasping the base of a perfectly proportioned white porcelain cup. The guest, in turn, receives the object of tradition and art with two folded hands and a slight nod of the head in appreciation of the respect shown. Korean architecture, interiors, art, and artifacts generate similar signs of appreciation and reverence for their natural world. Coupled with this is the Koreans' innate sense of beauty, which extends from the smallest object to the largest and allows them to create not only structures, interiors, and artifacts that are quintessentially Korean but also assimilate those of others so that they attain a Korean character. Such is the essence of "Korea style."

As a Westerner first visiting Korea, I misunderstood an architect when he pointed out the natural placement of a stone in front of a residence and said how beautiful it was because it was an old stone. Unwittingly, I asked how old he thought it was in geological time. He did not reply. To understand *his* meaning and desire to have an old stone, it is necessary to learn something of the teachings of a *seonbi*, a Korean philosopher from the Yi Dynasty (AD 1392–1910), better known today as the Joseon Dynasty, who taught that an old stone or rock represents age, not literal age, but a *respect* for age – respect for parents, teachers, and elders. The old rock has weathered many storms, seen the heat of summer, the bitter cold of winter. It is creased by water and smoothed by wind. It is not polished. It is not unrivalled by Western (or even Chinese and Japanese) standards, but viewed through Korean eyes it is perfect because of its reflection of age, nature, and sense of place.

Since antiquity Koreans have developed this special affinity with nature, an affinity which expresses itself in unmistakably Korean images of pastoral villages tucked between rocky mountains, forests of gnarled pine trees, lush green rice paddies, and walls and paths built with stones in their natural forms. Mountains form a pocket on the north and the Han River forms a soft, flowing line on the south of the 600-year-old capital city of Seoul. Early Neolithic remains found among the dolmens were placed in harmony with the natural landscape. During the Ancient Period (AD 200–600), houses evolved from pit dwellings to structures with earthen walls and thatched roofs, then to log structures, and finally to structures which showed the first evidence of the unique Korean raised floor panel heating system called *ondol*. It is believed that this heating system, which was to become so widespread in the seventeenth century, was never implemented in China because tables and chairs were used instead, and although floor seating did travel to Japan from Korea, the Japanese did not employ under-floor heating either. This technological innovation is still embraced by contemporary residential architecture for its energy efficiency, even distribution of heat, and elimination of the need for diffusers, radiators, and other visible mechanical devices. Under-floor radiant heating has since spread widely in the West and Japan.

The Three Kingdoms of the Ancient Period were brought together under the United Silla (seventh to tenth centuries), which absorbed the mature culture of the Tang Dynasty in China while developing a unique cultural identity. Buddhism and its art and architecture flourished during this period. In AD 918, the last king of Silla offered his kingdom to the ruler

Right Guests to Fashion Designer's Muse (page 50) enjoy lounging around the massive rough-edged granite slab table in the double-height living room, seated on floor cushions with accompanying cubicle armrests.

of Goguryeo, which took the name of Goryeo ("Korea" to Westerners). The Goryeo Dynasty (AD 918–1392) brought about a state embracing both Buddhism and Confucianism, and developed the ancient capital city of Songdo (now Gaeseong) in North Korea. The non-axial arrangement of the city responded to the natural contours of the mountainous landscape and led to the proclamation that nature should prevail over human design. Geomancy, a method of divination for locating favorable sites for cities, residences, and other activities, was proclaimed as a leading principle of design. The basic theory stems from the belief that the earth is the producer of all things and the energy of the earth in each site exercises a decisive influence over those who utilize the land. It is believed that when heaven and earth are in harmony, the inner forces will spring forth and the outer energies will grow, thereby producing wind and water; interestingly, the Korean word for geomancy, *pungsu*, literally means "wind and water." Principles of geomancy have been used to great effect in the orientation and design of Bedrock Manor (page 166) by Kim Kai Chun, and with the use of water elements, a leitmotif common to many of the residences in this book, notably those designed by Cho Byoungsoo, Choi Du Nam, and Kim Choon.

The basis of the architecture and art that we see today, and which forms much of contemporary "Korea style," was established during the Yi (Joseon) Dynasty, which supported the ideals and practices of Neo-Confucianism. The principles strongly influencing design at this time included dedication to simplicity, moderation, respect, and restraint. *Seonbi* also communicated the importance of writing, painting, meditation, and a minimalist approach to life which valued deep respect for all things natural. Pottery was simple yet exquisitely proportioned. Colors and decoration were minimized in both art and architecture, thus exposing the simplicity and purity of the materials. Simplistic perfection of man was sought as a counterpoint to the perfection of nature's complexities to achieve simplicity. In its ideal state, "Korea style"

Left All windows capture the sensuous outlines of the deep eaves, which, combined with the interplay of columns and beams inside, heighten the sensation of being inside a traditional Korean house (*hanok*) in Reincarnation of a Bygone Era (page 190).

values not only age and nature but also a commitment to minimalism as a way of life. These principles are employed to perfection in many of the design elements featured in this book, notably in the buildings designed by Cho Byoungsoo, Kim Incheurl, and Seung H-Sang.

Confucianism engendered a deep respect for all things natural, in particular for what their natural state might have been like without the intervention of man. This natural state found beauty in stones left unpolished, wood left unfinished, landscapes left untouched, and plants growing without stylistic shaping. The Korean culture discovered aesthetic and moral value within materials exposed to and thus altered by the natural elements. The sun bleaches and dries wood, the wind reshapes and textures both wood and stone, rain flows across surfaces gradually etching its path into the materials. Heat and cold expand and contract materials, reinforcing the aging process. All of these effects are evident in the highly esteemed vernacular complex, Masterpiece of Confucian Architecture (page 204).

The Korean concept of space has also been influential in its architecture and interior design. Historically, the spatial perception of Koreans differs dramatically from that of Westerners. When early Westerners first viewed traditional Korean landscape paintings and drawings, they found them flat and lacking in depth, shading, and realism. The Koreans, on the other hand, were astonished that Western landscapes looked so realistic, like mirror images, and were devoid of expressive brushwork and imagination. Unlike in the West, the function of traditional landscape painting in Korea was to act as a substitute for nature, allowing the viewer to wander imaginatively. The painting was meant to surround the viewer and provide no "viewing point" or pure perspective. This same principle can be observed in landscapes, courtyards, and other outdoor spaces surrounding buildings throughout Korea, and partly explains the importance to the Koreans of having a view, especially one facing a mountain. Likewise, while the

Japanese developed Zen gardens with purity and symbolism, the Korean culture continued to embrace natural expressions and the outdoors with much less formality. Trees, grass, and natural gardens are preferred to manicured and artificially developed landscapes. Grass, which has been browned by winter and the lack of water is considered more natural, and thus more beautiful, than the arranged perfection of raked sand. Trees, which reflect the effects of weather and time, are held to be more beautiful than a "tortured" bonsai.

Connections between nature and the indoors are important within most Asian cultures. Providing this connection, courtyards were developed as an essential design element throughout much of Asian architecture. While courtyards generally serve the same purpose all over Asia as a means of unifying the exterior and interior, they are culturally and architecturally treated quite differently. Traditional Japanese architecture employed *engawa* as a modulation space between the outside and inside, while Korean houses opened directly to the outdoors through a space called *daecheong*, where all doors were removed and hung under the eaves in the summer, as shown in Hanok Case Study (page 138) and Masterpiece of Confucian Architecture (page 204). *Daecheong* also served as multifunctional spaces that could be used for various domestic functions as well as a free-flowing space leading to the private rooms on its two sides. Metropolitan Sanctuary (page 18) and Maestro's Utopian Vision (page 174) incorporate both the open and free-flowing features of *daecheong*.

Korea faced difficult times during the global surge towards "modernism." Japanese occupation, the Korean War, and other geopolitical issues retarded the implementation of modernization in Korea. After the Korean War, Korean architecture and design languished for many years without strong leadership or definition. It was not until the principles of the modern movement were combined with the principles of Korean vernacular architecture that the content began to emerge as a distinctly Korean "style." Two of the most

Right Massive wooden columns placed in a zigzag pattern provide the sole support for the concrete slab roof in Square within a Square (page 212), harmonizing with the interior's natural materials and exposed concrete.

influential architects, Kim Joong-up and Kim Swoo-geun, emerged in the 1960s upon their return to Korea from studies abroad, at a time when economic progress was propelling a construction boom. In addition to introducing the International Style to Korea, they brought a sense of "architectural nationalism" to their designs because of their native Korean heritage. While the Western world looked to Leonardo Da Vinci in the sixteenth century and Le Corbusier in the twentieth century for proportional systems to create a more humane dimensioning system, Korean architects and designers turned to the ancient flexible module of *kan* and the measurements of *cheok*. The "organic" qualities of Korean modernism were probably first embraced by Kim Swoo-geun, as evident in Maestro's Utopian Vision (page 174) and Tribute to Korean Modernism (page 182), and remain as central design concepts for many of the architects/designers featured in this book.

As peace endured, Korea developed rapidly into an industrial base within the Pacific Rim and began to actively participate in the global economy. Beginning in the 1970s, a strong migration of many young, bright, and talented architecture and design students from Korea began traveling internationally to attend the world's most reputable graduate programs. At the same time, some prestigious programs within Korea began developing outstanding schools, which were strongly influenced internationally. Much of the international influence came from Korean faculty who attended graduate programs abroad and returned to practice and/or teach. These people are much more able to understand and express both theoretically and as built work contemporary architectural expressions which are informed and influenced by their traditions. This is especially true of the Yi (Joseon) Dynasty influence – integration of the arts and how houses become "galleries" for the display of cultural artifacts. Classic Korean objects, be they ceramic *kimchi* pots, *soban* tray tables, *dwiju* grain chests, or *hanbok* costumes – items that immediately distinguish themselves as being uniquely

Korean – are used with vernacular panache in interior decoration. Old rice cake boards are used as coffee tables, antique grain chests double up as storage for books and other household items, cushions are upholstered in Korean *moshi* linen and jewel-toned silks, and old stone mills and "ironing blocks" are used as garden "stepping stones." Similarly, stone figures once reserved for temples and royal burial mounds are displayed as modern-day *objets d'art*. "Korea style" is thus inextricably linked with art, craft, and architecture as showcased in Metropolitan Sanctuary (page 18), Lock Museum and Residence (page 28), Fashion Designer's Muse (page 50), Mountain Atelier (page 86), Folding Screen Mountain Retreat (page 116), Living with Art (page 128), and Collector's Hillside Haven (page 152).

Simplicity, moderation, constraint, and a deep respect for all things natural have remained the hallmarks of Korean architecture and interiors throughout the ages. Yet, despite maintaining these traditions, contemporary Korea is unique in its acceptance of contrast and lack of formality as part of its expression. Old is intertwined with new, rural with urban, unstructured with structured, noise with silence, and light with dark. "Korea style" often employs many of these contrasting elements to create uniquely harmonious relationships. Hanok Case Study (page 138) and Reincarnation of a Bygone Era (page 190) are classic examples of how old can be intertwined with new, while Kim Choon, Kim Kai Chun, and Seung H-Sang have a talent for contemporizing traditional tearooms. Portions of an old wall built in the Yi (Joseon) Dynasty for protection and definition around the city of Seoul emerge from the city perimeter at irregular intervals and provide for interesting relationships between old and new, as evidenced in Historical Stone Wall House (page 40) by Choi Du Nam. Square within a Square (page 212) shows the contrast between rural settings and urban designs, Mountain Atelier (page 86) exemplifies how unstructured elements can be combined with structured ones, and Reflex Penthouse

Left Elegantly curved pitched black *giwa* tiled roofs, dormers, and deep eaves are typical of traditional upper-class Korean houses, as exemplified in Hanok Case Study (page 138).

(page 146) demonstrates the contrast between noise and silence in a single space. Light and dark have once again been reintroduced into contemporary structures creating an ambience of mystery, subtlety, and reflection. Walls have transparency, translucency, and texture. Spaces have shade, shadow, filtered light, and moonlight. Papered screens, large overhangs, and movable walls all are historical precedents which contribute to contemporary expression. The Lock Museum and Residence (page 28), Fashion Designer's Muse (page 50), Folding Screen Mountain Retreat (page 116), and Tribute to Korean Modernism (page 182) all maximize the use of papered screens and filtered light. To the unobservant eye, these contrasts may appear strange and discordant, but within imperfection rests the perfection of nature.

As the world becomes more globalized, most countries are losing their architectural and cultural heritage to technology and expanded economies. National expressions of "style" and "substance" take a back seat to nondescript buildings and interiors which respond only to changing populations, limited budgets, and functionality. Some respond to this loss through mimicking or applying traditional images to pedestrian structures. The compromise reached often results in poor architecture and internal design that is neither contemporary nor traditional. Korea, however, has made significant gains in meeting the challenge of integrating tradition with contemporary architecture and interiors. Reaching a point where it can be identified as "Korea style" is significant. Through Korea's effort, other cultures may learn how to develop a style which reflects their own culture while meeting the demands of modernization. Korea's inclusive approach to design, integration of nature, and respect for heritage are important fundamentals for success. As this book shows, "style" is not necessarily shallow nor applied. It can mean substance, integration, and promise.

Right The Reflex Penthouse (page 146), a study in oblique angles and minimalist aesthetics, was an ingenious response to the site's physical and legal restrictions.

metropolitan sanctuary

DESIGNER KIM CHOON

This 210-square meter split-level house in Pyeongchang-dong, a residential district coveted for its proximity to downtown Seoul and to the natural wonders of Bukhan Mountain, is home to interior designer Kim Choon and his wife, a creative director, and their dog.

One goal in building the white stucco and Indian sandstone-clad residence in Pyeongchang-dong was to live in unison with the strong *gi* or primal force of the universe that this area is said to possess. The concept comes from the Five Elements School and Yin and Yang, which still play an important role in the lives of Koreans (see page 38). By recessing the house into the steeply sloping site, the designer has obtained harmony with the surrounding landscape, with the added benefit of privacy from neighbors. He also strongly believes that sub-ground structures are energy efficient as they are well insulated against the elements, subject of course to moisture-guard provided by double retaining walls. "I wanted a sanctuary to stimulate the five senses: music provided by the birds, open spaces with natural light, aromas from my wife's cooking, views of lush greenery, and a simple, easy-maintenance environment." The addition of an interior pool, one of the designer's signature features, also feeds the five senses.

Reminiscent of Korean vernacular architecture, the house is surrounded by courtyards. Three recessed court-yards, planted with maple trees, wisteria, and carpets of moss to ensure seasonal views, provide access at various levels as well as screening for each room. The house merges seamlessly with the courtyards because of the expansive use of glass. To withstand severe winter cold and condensation from the floor-heated interior, a double-glazed German window system was favored over frameless glass. The U-shaped spatial arrangement and the use of folding doors for individual rooms are reminiscent of the interrelated linear layout of traditional architecture. The dining room, with rooms built on either side, resembles the multipurpose space between the front and rear courtyards, called *daecheong*, in traditional Korean houses (see page 138). The individual rooms are enclosed yet airy since all doors and windows are left open much of the time to heighten the connection with the exterior.

While the courtyards are contained and intimate, the interior is spacious and bright. Exposed concrete floors, glass walls, blond wood, and pure white walls contribute to the home's contemporary minimalist ambience. At the same time, they reflect a traditional aestheticism that values minimalist shapes, overall effect, and balance over excessive attention to detail. The couple's enthusiasm for antiques, collectibles, and art knows no bounds, making this unassuming space an ideal setting in which to display their fascinating collections.

Above and right The living room glows in the late afternoon sun, softly filtered by a large maple tree planted in the upper courtyard. Clustered around a striking coffee table constructed from pieces of old pinewood rice cake boards, the crisply tailored canvas seating is offset by tasteful Korean antiques: *soban* tray tables (see page 157, below) and a rare zelkova wood steamer trunk. The trunk appears Western but is unmistakably Korean because of its lock design. The wooden figurines on top were discovered in a flea market in Beijing. A large sisal carpet defines the seating area. The massive fireplace with white marble surrounds, where three separate fires can be burned, dominates the entire south wall. In the central fireplace section, dragon andirons purchased for *feng shui* protection are, oddly, of French origin. The audio-visual system's towering B&W speakers are disguised behind screens high on the walls, while AR speakers rest in an opposite corner and on the roof of the teahouse. The blank wall above the fireplace functions as a projector screen. Spanning the entire length of the wall on the upper courtyard side, sturdy steel bookshelves support the couple's extensive collection of books and magazines. The catwalk above the shelves provides additional space for displaying a tall Thai Buddha and a Chinese birdcage collection, while also allowing for window maintenance.

Above Sandwiched between two courtyards, the focal point of the dining room is a narrow pool surfaced with black granite and lined with old millstones and blocks once used to "iron" laundry with wooden bats (see page 46). Crafted by the late Japanese friend and furniture maker Kimura Jiro, the customized dining table, paired with vintage bentwood chairs, is made of reclaimed zelkova wood hand rubbed with natural lacquer. A Jasper Johns "Crosshatch" silkscreen print and a Thai Buddha image are displayed next to a pair of striking French iron doors discovered in a New York architectural salvage shop. The table is set with hand-thrown porcelain inspired by the pure color and forms of the early Joseon period. Marei, a Tokyo-based design and restaurant consultant studio co-owned by the wife and a partner designer, created these for a restaurant project in Seoul.

Above The culinary-loving wife designed the functional details of the open-plan kitchen, which is finished in a palette of white – honed white marble countertop and white laminate cabinetry – with a rear back-up area. The stainless steel gas cooker top, oven, and dishwasher are from Neff, a German manufacturer. Conveniently at hand, dried foods and seasonings in glass jars make an interesting and colorful display on inset shelves. An opening in the back wall provides easy access to the kitchen counter from the rear back-up area. Designed to cover the entire kitchen area, the large hood efficiently absorbs all cooking fumes. Beam lamps above the grilles project fingertip lighting. The doorway at back leads to the walk-in closet located between the master bedroom and bathroom.

Below An antique stone frog, the shimmering flames of floating candles, and the soothing sounds of trickling water greet guests as they enter the dining room. Set with black pebbles, old millstones, and blocks once used to "iron" laundry with wooden bats, the pool, along with the moss-covered garden and kilim carpet, add textural interest to the exposed concrete dining room floor.

Right Installed on the opposite side of the spacious six-meter-high living room, the teahouse, another signature feature of the designer, provides an intimate and meditative space. Although the design incorporates contemporary strip lighting and other innovative features, and is without doors, it does contain vernacular elements such as papered walls, an oiled-paper *ondol* floor, pinewood borders, and round pillars (traditionally forbidden in private residences but often seen gracing old upper-class houses). A novel element is the tabletop floating above a sunken pit – inspired by those found in contemporary Japanese restaurants – to provide greater comfort to users than conventional floor seating with tray tables. The tabletop and its base block can be removed, and a hinged panel, set upright into the back wall, can be lowered flush to the floor. This versatile panel, oil-papered on the reverse to match the floor, allows traditional bedding stored in the closet paneled with old carved wooden doors on the right, to be laid on the floor. By lowering the woven bamboo screens, the teahouse becomes an extra guest room.

Above A collection of Baekje (18 BC–AD 600) and Unified Silla period (AD 668–935) earthenware is displayed under a large "Hollywood" acrylic on canvas by Kim Janghee. The pure shapes and combed patterns of the ancient Korean earthenware harmonize beautifully with the contemporary painting.

Right In order to keep the kitchen compact and tidy, the owner's extensive collection of tableware and bulky kitchen appliances, including a professional grade slicing machine and ice cream maker plugged in and ready to go, are stored in the rear pine-veneered floor-to-ceiling closet. Electric outlets have been provided in two different voltages, Korean and Japanese, because of the many Japanese-manufactured appliances in the kitchen.

Left An antique *soban* tray table embraces two old lacquered paper craft containers used for holding a literati-scholar's accouterments. Such containers were crafted in sets ranging from one to six. The starkness of the white canvas-upholstered armchairs is counterbalanced by eye-catching cushions covered in the famed Charles and Ray Eames "Small Dot Pattern."

Below With their ovoid bodies and graceful necks, the celadon liquor bottles on top of the *dwiju* grain chest on page 24 are in the classic shapes of *cheongja*. Although influenced by Chinese wares such as Ru, Ding, and Yue, the gray-green hue – coveted by the aristocracy and Seon (Zen) Buddhist monks who preferred it to white porcelain – and *sanggam* inlay are unique to the Korean peninsula.

Left Inspired by traditional Japanese aesthetics, the modern woven bamboo floor lamps are designed by Marei and made by a group of skilled Japanese artisans. The lamps replicate the linear shape of the adjacent antique *dwiju* grain chest, stripped to expose its natural blond color. *Dwiju* were constructed with four sturdy posts to support the weight of the contents. Straight-grained wood was used for the posts while panels of beautifully grained woods, such as the zelkova seen here, were employed for the front. A collection of late Goryeo Dynasty (AD 918–1392) celadon liquor bottles is displayed on top.

Above Framed by a roaring fire, a collection of burial horse clay figurines from an unknown period is a whimsical adornment on the pinewood slab coffee table set with champagne and finger food.

Right In a corner of the living room, a refined late Joseon-period ginko wood *soban* table holding a stack of antique dishes and art books, is paired with a large canvas floor cushion on a kilim carpet.

Left The linen closet in the bathroom, carved with flowing calligraphic works by the owner's father, is a reproduction of a traditional book-shelf-cum-cupboard. It is a good example of Korean furniture that is highly esteemed by local and international collectors for its simplicity of lines and planes, discreet use of metal hardware, and pragmatic design. Hinged doors not only pull open but also slide in either direction, allowing access to every corner of the cupboard. An early "Building" collage by Ohtake Shinro adorns the wall. Throughout the house, a personal, eclectic mix of objects throws period and contemporary pieces together, such as the stainless steel Alessi canisters, Chinese lacquered letterboxes, and Korean celadon ware seen on the hewn pinewood vanity counter. Unusually, everyday table wine is housed below.

Right and below A nineteenth-century zelkova wood *yakjang* – a medicine chest with a distinctive row of small drawers originally used to store medicinal herbs, and now toiletries – stands in front of a window looking out to a moss garden. A wood Thai Buddha on top is silhouetted against the light. An extraordinary life-sized reproduction of one of the famed Chinese Xian tomb terracotta soldiers and a light-installed Balinese offering house in the background are glimpsed through the window.

Above left and center The powder room is an ever-changing gallery for the couple's extensive collection of miniatures, such as the old Moroccan kohl containers shown here. An old pinewood rice cake board is fitted with a stainless steel basin and fixtures from Vola.

lock museum and residence
ARCHITECT SEUNG H-SANG

Above The building, constructed without the use of a single bolt, resembles a large rust-red box encased on all sides in uninterrupted sheets of Corten steel. To avoid leaving traces of welding on its surface, an innovative technique of welding the steel on the inner side was employed. A single box window punctuates the monochromatic façade. Perched on top of the monumental steel box is the glass box housing the living quarters. The building plan and its model was the first architectural work to be included in the collection of the National Museum of Contemporary Art in Korea.

Opposite Sliding papered latticed screens envelop the glass-walled residence and imbue the house with softly filtered light and a tranquil ambience. At night, the screens are fully opened to reveal the glittering city nightscape. The diagonal lines of the staircase leading to the upper mezzanine level add to the dynamic aesthetics of the house.

Daehakno, meaning "University Road," is an area in Seoul known for its art and youth culture. Often compared to Montmartre in Paris, it was originally the home of Seoul National University, Korea's most prestigious institution of higher learning. The expanding university has since moved to another location, but the street remains a popular hang-out for people from all walks of life. Many of the old residences have also disappeared due to the rapid commercialization of the area. Now, over forty theaters and concert halls, along with cafés and restaurants serving everything from authentic Korean barbecue to fast food, occupy the area.

Amidst this disjunctive urban landscape of old and new, Choi Hong-kyu chose to build a spectacular home for his family and beloved collection of over 3000 locks from Korea and abroad. Hailed as a modern-day blacksmith and the owner of a wildly successful architectural hardware store called Choigacheolmuljeom, Choi is an avid collector of Korean antiques and an expert on metalwork. He has single-handedly changed the perception of metal and metalworkers in Korea today. Committed to providing a huge selection of architectural hardware, he opened his shop in 1989 with five designers on the staff and a workshop where skilled blacksmiths turn out regular products as well as custom-designed pieces. He also runs a blacksmith school with the hope of reviving the art and craft of traditional metalwork.

A multifunctional building was required to house both the public (commercial and non-profit) and private spaces: a café on the ground floor, an antique shop and gallery on the second floor, the museum's temporary exhibition room on the third, a permanent collection on the fourth, and a residence on the fifth and sixth floors. "Most people regard metal as being cold and hard, but to me it is a warm and soft material with infinite potential to variegate. I wanted the building to express these qualities of metal." Deeply impressed by architect Seung H-Sang's work, especially his design for the headquarters of advertising company Welcomm, Choi commissioned him to design the Lock Museum Building with a vast floor area of 1600 square meters. The architect's philosophy is to allow the innate qualities of materials to express themselves. His signature material, untreated Corten steel, was employed for this project without the addition of other textures or finishes.

Duality similar to the hard/soft, cold/warm characteristics of metal is manifest in the inner design of the Corten steel enclosure: the paper-swathed glass box residence perched atop and the glass atrium inserted into its central core opening inner spaces to the sky. The architect refers to the atrium, which dissects the upper three floors of the building, as also being a device to orientate visitors within the dark museum. The unadorned architectural material defines the character of the building, allowing time and the elements to produce a protective patina of rust. In this building, the passage of time not only enhances the beauty of metal but also magnifies the historical value of the precious artifacts housed within.

Above The staircase railing extends around the mezzanine floor for visual continuity. Lined with built-in bookcases, the passageway leads to the master bedroom suite. A glass-enclosed courtyard provides plenty of sunlight and views from the family room, hallway, and master bedroom of a lush grove of black bamboo.

Left The top half of the central glass atrium is seen from the bridgeway located on the west side of the residence. A Corten steel planter is built along the outside of the inner corridor. The void below houses the moss-covered garden in the fourth-floor museum.

Right The pristine double-height living room features an entire wall of papered latticed screens. Designed by the owner, the minimalist coffee table adorned with a bowl of fragrant quinces was crafted in sandblasted stainless steel at his workshop. His portrait sits on the low pinewood bench at the far end of the room.

Right Highlighted by filtered light, the grid pattern of the screens and linear planes of the pinewood dining table and Corian kitchen counter create a stunning composition. The kitchen counter and cabinetry are all from the Spanish manufacturer Gamadecor.

Above Enamored by its wonderful aromatic and therapeutic qualities, the owner imported a *hinoki* (cedar) wood tub from Japan for the master bathroom. The *hinoki* bathroom is located off a long galley sink area, with a Corian counter and cabinets designed by the architect, which connects the master bedroom at one end and closet/storage spaces at the other.

Below left Box-framed antique pillow ends make beautiful displays on a shelf in the family room.

Below right A contemporary clay pot by ceramic artist Lee Heonjeong, placed in one corner, softens the linearity of the living room.

Above Built along the north side of the living and dining area, the terrace fulfills the owner's dream of a roof garden and water feature. A careful selection of Korean wildflowers and plants border the stone path. A white plastered "flower wall," typical of those developed in the sixteenth century to decorate the inside of stone boundary walls, contains delicate hand-molded and fired plum blossoms by artisan Suh Sanghwa, who restored the walls of Gyeongbokgung Palace.

Right A 150-year-old rice cake board serves as a coffee table in the up-stairs family room. Carved out of a single piece of pinewood, its concave center and short legs are characteristic of those found in the Tongyoung region of Korea.

Above A pair of lava stone tomb guardians from Jeju Island greets visitors as they enter the museum. The moss-covered garden on which they are placed is located at the bottom level of the atrium that dissects the upper three floors of the building.

Right Korean fish-shaped locks are generally in the shape of a Crucian carp. They symbolize success because of the expression "the fish turns into a dragon," fertility as fish produce many eggs, and protection as fish do not close their eyes even at night. The color blue refers to spring and is believed to ward off evil and bring prosperity.

Right Traditional Korean house gates opened inwards with a ring on the outside and a latch on the inside. Latches were often more symbolic than secure. This late Joseon-period gate latch is very realistic, with the growth rings of the wood used to depict the backs of the fish.

Below A streak of sunlight streams in from the small gallery in the back installed with windows.

Bottom Typical of all Korean locks, regardless of the period, a *hambak* lock features a round watermelon-like attachment in the center of a basic *deegut* (third letter of the Korean alphabet) shape. Made in the late Joseon period, it has a locking mechanism that is somewhat similar to modern-day locks.

Below The museum is designed as a labyrinth for visitors to "discover" treasures in the dark. Locks are encased in glass, like pieces of precious jewelry, dramatically highlighted with concentrated beams of narrow light. Lighting at the Gallery of Horyuji Treasures in Tokyo, designed by MOMA architect Taniguchi Yoshio, was a great source of inspiration for the owner when setting up this museum.

Below Curated and designed by the owner is an exhibition entitled "Locks of the World." The plastered panels on which the locks are mounted were painted in the five traditional colors of Korea. Called *obang saek*, the colors – blue, red, yellow, white, and black – symbolize the Five Elements as manifestations of Yin and Yang on earth (wood, fire, earth, metal, and water) necessary for balance and harmony. To have one element out of balance weakens both the mind and the body, and disrupts the flow of *gi* or primal force of the universe.

Above right At the owner's suggestion, glass walls were used in the museum's temporary exhibition hall to showcase his collection of pre-historic Baekje (18 BC–AD 600) and Silla (57 BC–AD 936) earthenware and stoneware. Floor-to-ceiling sliding panels are pulled closed when wall space is required inside the exhibition hall.

Below right A selection of typical Korean *hambak* locks.

historical stone wall house

ARCHITECT **CHOI DU NAM**

When it comes to designing their own homes, architects generally fall into two camps: those who test their design concepts by building for themselves and those who prefer to live in non-designed neutral environments. Home to architect Choi Du Nam, his attorney wife, and their two children was not only a test of the architect's design concepts but also a massive labor of love. The 165-square meter house has a complicated history, proven by a thick album of photographs and drawings compiled by the architect's wife, but it is also a celebration of her husband's persistence and creativity.

The story begins with the couple's desire to have a home within three kilometers of the wife's workplace in downtown Seoul, yet with a view of the Bukhan Mountain. The wife originally saw the site in Buam-dong – on which stood a dilapidated house – in the spring of 1999. "The steep and narrow roads immediately discouraged me from going any further, but feeling obliged to have a look for the sake of the realtor who took me there, I climbed to the roof only to discover this breathtaking mountain view and the remains of the historical stone wall" – the wall originally surrounding the entire medieval city of Seoul to protect its castle and city residents from foreign intruders.

The decision to acquire the house was made when the couple learned that the area was designated a green belt and that all new structures had to be built within the perimeters of existing buildings, thereby guaranteeing preservation of the lush natural surroundings and mountain view. The price was also within their budget. It was only after the sale that they discovered that part of the existing house had been built illegally on the neighboring lot. Initial plans to renovate the house proved impossible, leaving no choice but to rebuild. Six months were spent prior to this determining the legal boundaries. Compounding the difficulties was a preservation law requiring a distance of five meters from the house to the historical wall running lengthwise along the east side of the lot, with additional height restrictions prohibiting obstruction of the wall. After all subtractions, the legal building area was reduced to a mere 55 percent of the total lot size.

After drawing up countless plans addressing the obstacles, the architect finally plumped for a plan that capitalized on the beauty of the historical wall while maximizing the living areas in the narrow lot. The arc-shaped design of the exposed concrete structure is a perfect response to the narrow building area. The upper entry level houses the living, dining, and kitchen areas, son's bedroom, guest room, and bathroom. Located on the lower level are the family room-cum-master bedroom, master bathroom, daughter's bedroom, and garage. Having fulfilled all functional requirements, the architect then proceeded to design the features he personally wanted: water elements and a large roof deck for mountain viewing and entertaining.

Right The ivy-clad medieval wall running alongside the back of the upper level of the house is juxtaposed against a minimalist water element at its base: a narrow pool running the width of the lot. Pine trees and peonies, classic Korean images, harmonize beautifully with the historical wall. An unsightly retaining wall and concrete water tank thoughtlessly built against the historical wall by the former owners were demolished step by step. To compensate for the removed retaining wall and to provide extra moisture-guard, two new retaining concrete walls were constructed under the pond, hidden from view. The staircase built along this pond leads from the main gate to the upper-level entrance of the house and the roof deck on top. On top of the new retaining wall, the foundation for the new garden was built with old stone blocks acquired in an antiques market.

Opposite Encased in glass and sandblasted stainless steel with limestone surrounds, the see-through fireplace acts as a divider between the living and dining areas. Designed by the architect himself, the steel coffee table is paired with large cushions upholstered in jewel-toned Korean silks, made by Mono Collection. The floor seating is ideal for enjoying the fireplace and for maximizing the space in the small living room. The collage on the wall is assembled from seashells collected by the children on a summer holiday in Martha's Vineyard. Sunlight flooding in from the skylight provides additional heat in the winter but is tempered by electronically controlled shades in the summer.

Above To maximize space in the small house, the family sleeps on traditional hand-dyed silk bedding on the heated Cabruva wood floor. Deeply impressed by the jewel-toned colors of silk bedding displayed at Unhyeongung Palace, the wife was able to obtain similar custom-made bedding with the help of a traditional bedding shop. The couple sleeps in the area behind the lower-level family room, which is partitioned for privacy at night with a heavy cotton-faced silk curtain. The children have their own bedrooms and bathrooms. The armchairs in the family room are modeled on a leather sofa the couple bought in Boston when they were newlyweds, scaled down for the ergonomics of the Asian physique. A coffee table was designed in black leather to match.

Left Throughout the house, innovative design maximizes the space. Opposite the entrance, the guest room-cum-music room for the guitarist son can be partitioned with a set of folding doors, which are normally kept open. A collection of Goryeo Dynasty (AD 918–1392) celadon ware is displayed on the glass shelf below.

Below The Bukhan Mountain forms a splendid backdrop to the dining area. Suspended above the dining table, designed by the architect, the lighting fixtures are classics from the 1980s by Ingo Maurer.

Above right The skylight above the entrance hall is fitted with electronically controlled shades.

Below right The Bulthaup kitchen, equipped with a high-calorie gas stove, is where the busy attorney and mother of two indulges in her love of cooking and entertaining. She meticulously sketched all details of the kitchen, including the position of electric outlets in the appliance garage in two different voltages, local and US. For efficient workflow, the kitchen counter is equipped with a washer/dryer, and the internal staircase connecting the two floors is placed next to the kitchen, making it convenient for carrying groceries from the lower-level garage.

Left An antique iron charcoal brazier and kettle are used for boiling water to serve tea to guests at the coffee table.

Below An old ceramic Chinese paperweight adds interest to the living room shelf.

Above An exquisite traditional stone "ironing" block, used to beat the wrinkles out of laundry with wooden bats, is given the attention it deserves in front of the roaring fire.

Above Enhanced by a carpet of brilliant green duckweed and a stone turtle, a Chinese stone water bowl from the Han Dynasty (202 BC–AD 220) greets visitors in the entrance hall.

Above A tasteful display of Gaya Federation (AD 42–56) earthenware sits atop the shoe closet in the entrance hall. The medieval stone wall and water feature are visible beyond.

Left The house sits elevated above the street on an old retaining wall. A sandblasted steel gate opens to the arced-shaped exposed concrete structure fitted with double-paned aluminum-framed windows.

Right A precast concrete paneled wall encloses the lower garden planted with Chinese trumpet creepers, spreading junipers, and maples. Old stone blocks are used to create a walkway laid in an arced pattern that traces the shape of the building.

Right Flanked by two grape vines trained to stand upright, the water element at the end of the walkway is made from old stone blocks.

Far right A close-up of the sand-blasted steel gate which opens to the exposed concrete house.

Below To accommodate the large number of guests who frequent the house, the spacious roof deck, paved in *moabi*, an Indonesian wood, and gravel, has two seating areas. Two circular zinc-plated planters contain summer vege-tables and herbs, replanted annu-ally. The large *kimchi* pot hides gardening tools. A steel kennel (not shown) in the upper garden was specially designed by the architect for the family dog.

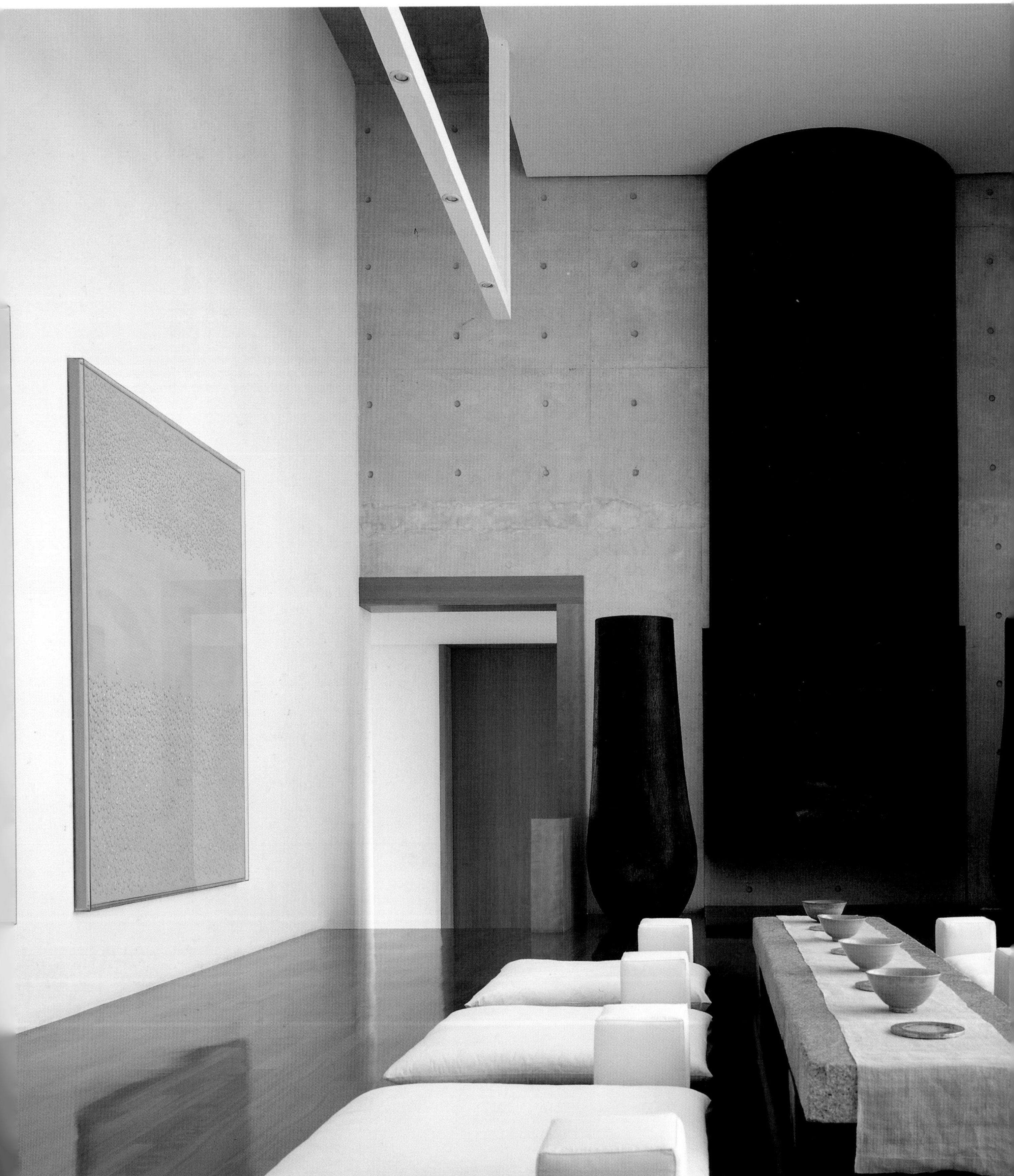

fashion designer's muse

DESIGNER **LEE CHONG-HWAN**

UN Village in Hannam-dong is one of the oldest post-Korean War residential projects in Seoul. Masterminded in the late 1950s by the then president, Rhee Syngman, to provide a European ambience and a modern lifestyle for United Nations military officers, the houses in the exclusive enclave were eagerly snapped up by diplomats and foreign businessmen as well as wealthy Koreans. Today, UN Village remains a popular spot for embassies and ambassadors and the well-to-do.

In 1998 eminent fashion designer Jin Teok rebuilt this residence after her original house on the same site was tragically destroyed by fire. The original house, which she had purchased and renovated, was the twentieth house to be built in the area. Having resided in several different parts of the city, the fashion designer decided to move here for the stunning views of the Han River and because of its proximity to the Gangnam area across the river where her offices are located.

The three-story building, which has a generous floor space of 696.54 square meters, is composed of three square sand-brushed concrete volumes. The various rooms in the residence are separated into two wings connected by a central block housing the stairwell. The larger wing, occupying the west section, contains the double-height living room and powder room on the ground floor, and quarters for an unmarried son, a library, and a terrace on the upper levels. The east wing houses the kitchen and dining room on the ground floor, and quarters for a married son and his family and the master bedroom suite on the upper levels.

"I wake up every morning to inspiring views of the river and city skyline. One of my favorite ways to relax in the summers is tending the water lilies and floating grass on my terrace. But I enjoy the house in every season, rain or shine, night or day. It is very contemporary and minimalist in design but there is a soothing Asian spirituality flowing within. I guess that's mostly because the designer is Korean."

Interior designer Lee Chong-hwan's association with the owner goes back more than twenty years, during which time he has designed all the owner's boutiques, offices, and former residences. Lee, who has a background in theater, believes in designing spaces with slightly less than what is required, thus allowing the occupants to add the finishing touches themselves. In this house, he concentrated on an interplay of varying volumes, surfaces, and materials while making sure the owner was able to imbue the spaces with her own creative touch.

Left The exposed concrete on the outside of the house continues into the interior of the double-height living room, raised by five steps above the rest of the ground floor to capture views of the river. Colossal sliding latticed doors and a dramatic black steel tower enclosing a fireplace, flanked by two monumental Thai wooden vases, add considerable drama in the modernist space. Preferring to sit on the heated, highly glossed Doussie Afrikan wood floor rather than on Western-style sofas, the owner designed a long, low table, floor cushions, and cubicle armrests for entertaining her guests. The massive scale of the rough-edged granite slab table is a wonderfully appropriate response to the other elements in the room. Down lights installed behind the lowered wall on the west side and in the sculptural steel beam provide evening lighting, controlled with a Lutron dimming system programed with a choice of four different light moods. A pair of Kim Tschang-yeul's famed water drop paintings dominates the north wall.

Left A towering black steel fireplace dominates the east wall of the living room. A slab of polished black granite placed on the Doussie Afrikan wood floor catches ashes from the open hearth. The monumental Thai wooden vases standing by the fireplace were purchased in Paris.

Right A study in black and white, the elegant dining room is furnished with ebony-stained oak wood furniture from Casa Milano. The pendant light fitting above the table is from Vetri Murano. Favorite pieces from the owner's extensive collection of tableware and linens are stored in the cabinet adorned with a Chinese-inspired lock plate. A late Joseon-period (1392–1910) white porcelain vase with a floral design in blue underglaze *cheonghwa baekja* sits atop (see page 147). The matching ebony-stained oak console is dressed with sleek chrome candlestands, antique tea bowls, and a modern cross. To the left, a corner section outside the dining room (not visible here) is devoted to a collection of old ceramic chimneys.

Below The colossal sliding latticed doors, papered on the outside in contrast to the Korean vernacular style, open to views of the Han River. Plastic armchairs made by MDF of Italy are imported by Te Home, a home furnishings store belonging to the owner's two sons.

Above The third-floor landing flows into a library facing a large terrace decked with wenge wood on which stands a collection of old *onggi* pots (see page 164). A bookshelf fitted with a rolling ladder houses the owner's collection of fashion and photography books. The Wooden Chairs, designed by Marc Newson in 1992 for Cappellini, are both practical and elegant. Cove lighting in the ceiling adds a warm accent in the evenings.

Left A stark white hallway leads to the west wing bedroom suite occupied by the single son. The designer's meticulous attention to detail is reflected in the recessed closed doors that lie flush with the walls, creating a clean, uninterrupted surface. The penthouse library is seen above.

Right A series of bold lithographs complements the staircase leading to the third-floor master bedroom suite and library. The balustrades are made of clear glass and fitted with brushed stainless steel pipes that appear to be suspended in mid-air. Fixed glass windows run top to bottom on the west wall, allowing dynamic views of the city.

Left An antique folding screen forms an attractive divider between the kitchen and dining area. In a traditional house, the number of panels varied according to the size of the rooms. Those adorning the female quarters were mostly painted with flowers and birds whereas those made for the male quarters were painted with land-scapes, scenes from a scholar's room (see page 93), or of everyday life. Korean manufacturer Hanssem, for whom the interior designer worked many years ago, produced the kitchen furniture. The coun-tertop is finished in white Corian, while the appliances are from German manufacturer Neff and US firm General Electric.

Left, above, and right The low table in the living room is a rough-edged granite slab supported on two wooden "ironing" blocks. A collection of antique bowls lines this table, along with silver-rimmed glass dishes purchased on a trip to Morocco. Japanese tea masters coveted the unique beauty of utilitarian Korean bowls, prais-ing the colors of Goryeo celadon and the natural forms and surfaces of sixteenth-century *ido* ware. Some of these were later designated as national treasures in Japan when Japanese forces returned home with numerous Joseon potters and their ceramics after the invasion of Korea in 1592. What fascinated the Japanese was the quiet elegance and forms of the commonplace bowls. The table runner, cushions, and cubicle armrests are made with Korean *moshi* hemp. Fruit is served on a large hand-thrown ceramic platter.

Above and left After long hours at work, the paper-floored penthouse master suite is an oasis of calm. A stylish mixture of furnishings graces the room. Standing behind the contemporary platform bed is an antique brush-and-ink folding screen painted with Korean birds and flowers. Such a screen, consisting of two to twelve panels, was an essential yet artistic item in the traditional home because of its unlimited versatility. It was used as a windscreen, room divider, a piece of art in itself, or headboard in a bedroom, as seen here. Subject matter ranging from Chinese characters, flowers and birds, the ten creatures of longevity, peonies, and even aphorisms or poetry, was rendered in paintings, calligraphy, and embroidery. A folding screen formed a backdrop to important rites of passage: first birthday, marriage ceremony, passing of a state examination, seventieth birthday, and funeral. The sculpturesque luminaries handcrafted from rolls of crinkled paper were love at first sight and were shipped from Milan. Aromatic candles placed on unique resin-infused macramé cubes scent the room to soothe the weary soul. A dramatic night scene of the Dongho Bridge and city traffic unfolds in front of the window.

Right The ethereal powder room, surfaced with Emperado marble, showcases the designer's hallmark detailing founded on a system of grids. Reveals installed with recessed lighting separate the planes of the ceiling, wall, and floor. The vanity counter is fitted with a floating glass sink from Vola. Vivid rose-colored potpourri along the counter top and on a square white plate below the basin, adds visual spice as well as ambrosial scent to the long, narrow room.

Above A large soaking tub, finished in Emperado marble, is installed in the center of the master bathroom. A glass-enclosed shower booth lies behind. Spanking white linens appoint the bathroom as in the rest of the house. The adjoining dressing room allows ample storage for the owner's extensive wardrobe.

Right On the right of the house, the floor of the glass-encased entrance area is surfaced with gray ceramic tiles, while the door is veneered in cherry wood. Tassels are hung as part of a "Moroccan" theme; the owner redecorates the house frequently according to her current inspirations. On the left, the double-height living room is visible through its opened papered screens.

glass house

ARCHITECT **CHOI DU NAM**

Located on a spectacular estate in Gonjiam, a rural area south of Seoul known for its forested mountains and natural spring waters, the Glass House symbolizes the owners' passion for gardening and their life-long dream of dining amongst flowers. The entrepreneur-artist couple had initially commissioned a greenhouse engineer to design their dream home but after reviewing the proposed plans realized that input from an architect was necessary.

After surveying the immense grounds, architect Choi Du Nam decided that the house would be best located on a slope halfway between the mountains and an existing residence. In line with the views of many of his contemporaries concerned with Korean vernacular styles, he also decided that the structure should blend with the terrain, with minimal impact on the natural surroundings, but at the same time be an autonomous structure. To satisfy the clients' request for a greenhouse-style home – a largely transparent structure reminiscent of the celebrated "glass boxes" of master architects Mies van der Rohe and Phillip Johnson – Choi opted for an arced glass enclosure wrapped around a solid mass covered with fieldstone, duplicating the materials of the old residence.

Although the structure of the 187-square meter Glass House is relatively simple – a steel frame constructed around a concrete core – the mechanics of controlling the humidity, heat, and solar requirements for human and plant life were a challenge to the architect and he was forced to seek the expertise of an HACV (heating, air conditioning, ventilation) engineer. Floor heating, air conditioning, and an electronic system for opening and closing the skylight were installed to provide comfort for the occupants and their plants throughout the four seasons. The year-round supply of luxuriant flowering plants for both the Glass House and the huge surrounding garden comes from another working greenhouse built behind the main structure, where plants are seeded and cultivated. The couple has also designed wildflower, water, vegetable, and herb gardens within the extensive grounds. "Our life here is remarkably simple – discussing dinner menus, harvesting herbs and vegetables, gathering wild flowers, and selecting the tableware for entertaining our friends and family," comments the busy entrepreneur.

The estate includes the original thirty-year-old residence that the owner built for his late father. Additional buildings have been added over the years to create an interesting complex of Tuscan-inspired fieldstone buildings with terracotta tiled roofs. These include a ceramic workshop to produce tableware for the owner's hotel projects, a gallery to house his collection of antiques and ceramics, a stable for livestock, a silo converted into a sauna, and an annex for traditional family ceremonies and gatherings. The owner's love for Europe and Africa has inspired many of the details seen throughout these buildings. The site also provides the couple with opportunities to experiment with landscaping ideas before implementing them on a grander scale in various projects.

Left The bold, minimalist glass-and-steel structure stands in the far corner of the manicured grounds. The monumentality of the building blends surprisingly well with the lush mountainous background because of its transparency and circular shape. The aluminum-framed double-paned window system was custom-built for the residence. Visible behind the pine tree, the fieldstone wall was newly constructed to harmonize with the exterior of the exiting residence.

Right Integrated as it is into the sloping land, the Glass House can be approached on two different levels. The architect, known for creating transitional entrance "pauses," designed a descent of a few steps at the lower-level entrance and an extended pathway from the old residence at the upper-level entrance. The lower entrance area seen here is paved in fieldstone whereas the floor of the interior is covered in slate. The lower row of windows can be opened during the day to provide air circulation for the plants.

Opposite Flooded with natural sunlight, the den on the mezzanine level is a favorite spot to sketch garden plans. The L.S.W. sofa designed by Philippe Starck in 1999 as a multifunctional – relax, read, work, and nap – piece of furniture, is placed in the perfect location for its enjoyment. It is harmoniously paired with the 254 Zap coffee table designed by Piero Lissoni.

Above Butterflies flock to the flower-filled Glass House. An Eastern Black Swallowtail rests on the glass top of the shower curtain rail in the bathroom adjoining the bedroom on the second floor. The smoothness of the floor, finished with Bianco marble, is a delightful contrast to the textured travertine mosaic tiles on the walls. The mirror is encased in a sandblasted steel frame, a signature feature of the architect's work.

Above right A glass railing installed within a sandblasted steel frame borders the mezzanine-level den and adjoining bedroom and bathroom. The transparency allows a free flow of space between the two levels. The vivid mesh and stainless steel Nxt chairs and table manufactured by Brown Jordan were purchased to complement the purple flowers filling the Glass House.

Right Located between the ceramic workshop and the old residence, a traditional silo has been converted into a Korean sauna. The floor can be heated to the required temperature by adjusting the amount of wood fed into its exterior fire pit. Unlike Scandinavians, Koreans enjoy these rooms when lightly clothed, not only as a place to warm up but also as a room in which to relax and nap.

Left The Korean sauna is simply furnished with an antique brass candlestand, modern celadon ware, and a floor cushion.

Above Originally used for storing clothes and valuables, a *jang* chest from the late Joseon period (AD 1392–1910), with elegant inverted ends, makes an interesting composition with a Robert Mapplethorpe work in the living room of the old residence.

Right Massive porcelain dishes glazed in black, white, and celadon were designed by the artist of the house and are produced in the ceramic workshop on the estate. The stacked dishes are reminiscent of the geometric forms of Korean noblemen's hats woven from fine horsehair.

Left An alfresco seating area, one of several in the grounds, was created behind the old residence to accommodate some aluminum and teak furniture the owners purchased in Los Angeles. Surrounded by mature pine trees, hosta, bamboo grass, and a pond filled with water lilies, it is a perfect spot for afternoon tea. Home-made soy sauce, bean paste, and chili paste are stored in the *onggi* ceramic pots on the landscaped slope (see page 164).

Right Wooden steps bordered by fieldstone paving lead to the extended pathway connecting the old residence to the Glass House. Filled with nooks and crannies created by the various buildings, the large grounds have a multitude of paths and scenery to enjoy.

Below left The traditional cooking stove fueled by wood is still in use at the old residence. Cauldrons of hearty beef soup and rice are cooked here for the family and the large number of staff needed to keep the grounds in perfect condition and for the ceramic workshop.

Below Tropical water lettuces thrive year round in the warm temperatures of the Glass House.

Bottom A *seokdeung* stone lantern with Buddhist origins (see page 154, below), signifying enlightenment and rebirth, stands in the shade of an old pine.

treasure trove

Upon finding that the steep garden steps leading up to his former residence were becoming a challenge to his aging mother, haute couturier Suh Junggi moved to this condominium, situated directly on the south bank of the Han River, on Christmas Day 2002. Suh, whose creations are tailored for the *crème de la crème* of Korean society, and his fashion powerhouse executive wife, selected this place for its magnificent views of the Youngdong Bridge and city skyline.

Also known for his exquisite taste in art and antiques, the couturier admits to having caught "collector's fever" during his student days in New York and Paris. Returning to Seoul in 1990 to open his own salon after a successful career at New York fashion houses following his graduation from the Fashion Institute of Technology, Suh continued to frequent the local antique markets, sometimes as often as two or three times a week. "From the early days, I realized that Korean antiques had already become quite rare and pricey while Chinese antiques were still very accessible. So I naturally started to collect Chinese objects, especially imperial jade, which have always been my favorite. My mother also had reservations about keeping old Korean objects previously owned by strangers. Although Korean antiques furnished the *sarangbang* (see page 93) in my former residence, I decided to put them into storage, with the idea of using them in a country home in the future, and to decorate this apartment with my Chinese pieces and contemporary art."

The couturier has succeeded in creating a highly personal and stylized gem out of this contemporary condominium. The finishings – creamy marble floor accented with touches of black marble and rosy wood parquet and limestone walls – in the condominium have been carefully selected to create a neutral palette for the various collections. Every object and its arrangement reveal Suh's meticulous attention to detail and hold a wealth of information and memories. The centerpiece of the living room – referred to as his "playground" – is a brilliant collector's solution: a simple white platform for staging ever-changing collages.

Right Purchased in Shanghai, a pair of late Ming Dynasty (AD 1368–1644) lacquer-painted pigskin armoires dominates the east wall of the living room. Reproduction rosewood Chinese Ming chairs and a cornel dogwood branch arranged in a Korean Hweryeong "tear-drop" running glaze vessel sits in front. Hamilton modular sofas designed by Rodolfo Dordoni for Minotti wrap the north and west sides of the living room, accentuated by cushions upholstered in geometrically patterned Kuba cloth (once used as currency amongst the Bakuba of the Congo).

Left Molded glass Ghost chairs designed by Cini Boeri and Katayanagi Tomu (1987) flank a Chinese mother-of-pearl inlaid table. The man's imperial robe from the Qing Dynasty (AD 1644–1912) hanging on the wall is embellished with a "Mandarin chain" worn by nobility during Manchurian rule in China. The three strands of chameleon amethyst beads represent the wearer, his ancestor, and his mother.

Right and below The focus of the living room – the couturier's "playground" – is a Japanese Edo-period (AD 1603–1867) burled wood writing desk resplendent with antique Chinese calligraphy accouterments – a jade water dropper, porcelain ink brush pots, a silver inlaid iron box, a jade brush rest, apple green jade brushes, old calligraphy books (below left) – along with art books, an Edo-period iron candlestand, a Tibetan bronze pagoda, a stone Taoist deity figure, a miniature garden planted in an antique marble planter, and a Moroccan burled wood tray arranged with a coral branch, bird feathers and potpourri (below right).

Left In the niche of a storage unit swathed in crocodile-grain imprinted leather is an exquisite Buddhist stone tablet from the Han Dynasty (206 BC–AD 220), a birdcage, and an old scholar's stone. A dried coral-like branch from a bouquet casts a dramatic shadow on the ceiling. An old bronze urn filled with wild orchids, a rare iron candlestand, and a pair of vintage porcelain garden stools, all of Chinese origin, complete the picture.

Above In the cozy dining room, swathed with luscious silk and velvet drapes, a sculpture entitled "Before The Word There was Light, After The Word There Will Be Light" (1992) by the late illustrious Nam June Paik, sits atop a late Joseon-period Korean *sung sunggi* chest (see page 171). Fitted with a digital mechanism that can be reconfigured with original messages, the words "Bon Appetite" and "Welcome to Chez Mi and Jung, Love Forever" are spelt out in this household.

Right The small yet functional kitchen is fitted with German SieMatic cabinetry and Gaggennau and Miele appliances, including a built-in espresso machine. A pair of precious Han Dynasty (206–220 BC) terracotta burial figures sits atop the black marble counter. A still-life sculpture by George Segal with Suh's personal addition of an orchid is a tactile and visual delight on the center island. Like many other residences featured in this book, a separate kitchen (not shown) for preparing Korean dishes is built to the right.

Right Finished in brushed velvet-like wallpaper imported from France, the walls of the den serve as a showcase for prized works of art. Three Eduardo Chillida prints hang behind the desk, a generic console refinished with crocodile-grain imprinted leather. Next to the window is a pygmy bed and wooden crocodile figure, wedding gifts from the couturier's sister, a collector of African art, and cushions found in Cebu.

Below left Video art by Nam June Paik sits in the opposite corner while a Keith Haring plate, Mauro Staccioli sculpture and drawing, Choi Man Lin sculpture, and Kim Sun Rae wax paper work are displayed on the bookshelf amongst aesthetically stacked fashion and photography books.

Below right A nineteenth-century Chinese ancestral painting hangs in the cozy guest bedroom. On the bed are antique porcelain pillows and cotton-quilted pillows designed by the couturier with panels of vintage fabric.

Left The silk furnishings in the master bedroom – the bedding, cushions, and wall panels – were also designed by the couturier. Peony motifs from the traditional Korean wedding screen, originally worked in brilliant reds and pinks, are here in three shades of ivory thread on black silk, specially commissioned in China. Alabaster lamps and family photos sit on vintage Korean *ham* chests, traditionally used to carry gifts to a bride's house.

Above Adjacent to the master bathroom is an opulent powder room designed by the couturier for his wife. The black marble and rosewood dressing table, appointed with a Chinese antique mother-of-pearl inlaid lacquered mirror and shelves, vies for attention with vintage beads and imperial jade snuff bottles. A pair of vases decorated in *famille rose* enamels (first introduced in the Chinese Yongzheng period (AD 1723–35) for use on export porcelain ware), sits on wall shelves.

Right A pair of impressive Jin Dynasty (AD 1115–1234) Yue funerary jars flanks the silk-draped entrance to the walk-in closet. Serving to house the souls of the deceased without a proper burial, these urns were elaborately carved with human figures that summoned and cared for the wandering soul while palatial architectural details and animals are blessings for wealth and happiness in the next life.

Below "Self-portrait" by Nam June Paik sits at one end of the entrance hall. An exquisite antique Chinese bench, a pair of stone lion guardians, and a candle placed in an old Korean stone mortar add personal touches to the narrow, utilitarian space.

Clockwise from top left An eclectic array of objects on the dining table: woven rush placemats, antique Japanese lacquered plates, fish chopstick rests, and a long ceramic plate accentuated with orchids and silver Christofle birds. A scholar's stone, a coral Buddha figurine, an old scroll (shown), and a Korean stone box in a corner of the guest room. A collection of old *hyanghap* (turned wood Korean incense pots) on a tray table in a corner of the living room. Pages from a volume originally belonging to the couturier's grandfather of works by the renowned late Joseon-period calligrapher Kim Jeong-hee (1786–1856) sandwiched between two sheets of glass behind an oversized Chinese lavender jade snuff bottle.

poetry of wire

ARCHITECT CHO BYOUNGSOO

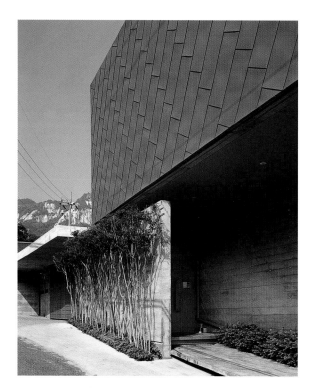

Above Finished with galvanized steel plates and exposed concrete imprinted with pinewood formwork, the street-side façade has been purposely kept low lying and restrained. An industrial-looking sloped concrete gangplank bordered with juniper bushes leads to the main gate. The sensation of openness and calm only begins inside the gate, where an expansive view of the eastern peaks of Bukhan Mountain can be had. Chinese trumpet creepers soften the outside wall.

Opposite Although the wife had initially asked for one large garden which she could fill with Korean wildflowers, white birch trees, moss, and treasured rocks from her father-in-law's garden, the architect, in response to the sloping terrain, created upper and lower gardens to capitalize on different views from each level of the house.

The owner of this sensational 584-square meter residence in Pyeongchang-dong (see page 18) is CEO of the second largest wire manufacturer in the world, a 25-year-old joint venture with a firm in Luxemburg. The company exports wires all over the world for automobile tires and for large-scale projects such as stadiums and bridges.

In designing any residence, architect Cho Byoungsoo believes that the structure should be kept as simple as possible while its relationship with the surroundings should be complex. To him, the heart of residential design lies in meeting the needs of the domestic rituals of daily life: eating, sleeping, and bathing. Thus, the design process for this house, located on the south side of a steeply sloping site, began by creating three separate zones according to the individual needs of the owner, his wife, and their two children. The architect then studied how the respective zones could relate to one another as well as to the surrounding views and to the site itself.

The client and his wife had originally asked that the house face south on an east–west axis, an orientation favored by most Koreans and which, in this case, allowed for a relatively large garden. This orientation, however, had two serious drawbacks: unfavorable light and views at the basement level and difficulty in establishing a natural relationship between the house and garden. An eastern orientation along a north–south axis – the north side closed to the road and the south side opened towards the view – was suggested as an alternative and was quickly agreed upon. On the ground level, utilitarian spaces such as the main gate, garage, front door, kitchen, and powder room are placed to the north, forming a buffer between the house and street. The more socially interactive spaces such as the living room, dining area, and outdoor deck are placed to the south against a wide-open view of Inwang Mountain. The basement level contains the more private spaces, such as a traditional *ondol* room facing the water garden, an audio-visual entertainment room, a library, and a wine cellar. The second floor houses the family room and three bedrooms. These spatial arrangements allow each zone to be defined by its individual character and by what the architect refers to as an "organic" flow between the zones. The result is a spectacular horizontal stratum of masses punctuated with signature design features, cantilevered stairs, skylights, and ribbon windows. Describing the spatial layout of the residence, the wife says: "We enjoy alfresco dining until as late as November. It's truly wonderful that we also have the luxury of choice of where to dine – on the deck on the ground floor with its wonderful mountain view or on the terrace next to the water garden below."

A dramatic "poetry of wire" spanning some 11 meters is the main focus of the interior. Nothing other than the structural walls at both ends and six 22-mm-thick wire cables, capable of holding two tons of tension per meter, support the bridge. Stainless steel channels on the underside of the bridge regulate the curve of the wires. Many types of wire were tested for the weight load of the bridge, the architect eventually choosing industrial PC (Precast Concrete) wire for its matte gray finish, over stainless steel wire that would have been the usual choice in this sort of application.

Below A combination of warm and neutral colors and textures was selected to furnish the living room, the heart of the residence for the four-member family who entertain frequently. The linen-upholstered Sidney sofa and armchairs are from Casa Armani. Two Barrel chairs designed by Frank Lloyd Wright sit in front of the fireplace.

Opposite left A detailed view of the bridge construction shows the curved bow-like tension of the wires threaded through stainless steel channels installed midway on the underside.

Opposite right The concrete fireplace surrounds are cast with an indent for storing logs, a thoughtful detail found in many of the architect's works.

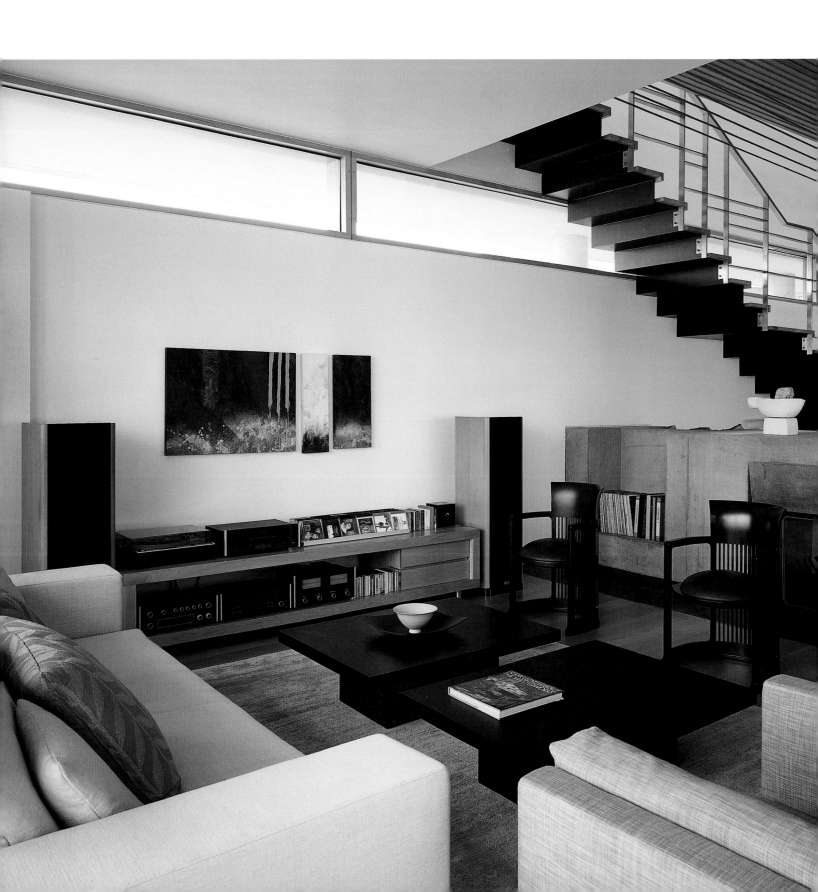

Above A massive exposed concrete fireplace divides the double-height ground floor into living and dining areas. The concrete surrounds have been cast with two indentations, one to house prized LP records from the owner's youth on the living room side and the other to store logs on the dining room side. A long ribbon window running alongside the cantilevered staircase allows for a cropped view of the revered Bukhan Mountain. Oak wood parquet flooring, 10 mm thick, was used throughout the house to resist warping from the floor heating. The dining table, custom-designed with a solid coconut wood tabletop crafted by the owner's friend in Indonesia, placed on top of polished steel legs, is paired with Cab chairs designed by Mario Bellini. Above it hangs the whimsical Plume chandelier by Baccarat embellished with interchangeable clear and red crystal drops.

Right The master bedroom wing and daughter's wing are located at opposite ends of the wire bridge. A walk-in closet installed behind the left wall stretches along the entire length of the bridge, connecting the two wings within the closet. The staircase and wall are animated by natural light flooding in from the narrow skylight installed above the dropped ceiling. A leather and fiber woven material insulated with a sponge padding has been applied to both sides of the bridge railing to provide acoustic absorption in the exposed concrete interior. An octal series by Götz Diergarten is seen under the bridge alongside the stairs leading to the basement level.

Right An ipe wood deck wraps around two sides of the living and dining area. The bottom half of the fir wood window frame is zinc-clad on the exterior for protection against water damage. Three exposed concrete columns support the eaves of the covered decks. Seating for alfresco dining is provided by the classic Le Corbusier dining table paired with funky acrylic Louis Ghost chairs designed by Philippe Starck. Cutouts in the exposed concrete wall are examples of the architect's favored "editing" of views.

Opposite The living room behind the massive fireplace faces south to expansive views. Large windows framed in beautifully crafted fir wood surround the south and east sides of the living/dining areas. A Cab bench designed by Mario Bellini sits next to the log bin set in the concrete fireplace.

Above and left The *ondol* (see page 138) room in the basement is a sublime, meditative space suffused with soft light filtered through papered screen doors. It is appointed with modern-day reproductions of traditional furnishings as well as antiques. The *boryo* day bed-like cushion is a modernized piece upholstered in jewel-toned silk. The tray table placed in front is also a reproduction. Antique bookshelves and *mungap* for storing writing supplies line the left wall, as in the layout of the traditional study. Two sets of papered screen doors slide open to the water garden below, designed to be viewed from the low vantage point, and cropped views of the white birch tree stems and sky above.

Left A pair of water-filled sculptures called *mulhwak* adds visual interest to the dining area on the outside deck. Created by sculptor Lee Young-hak, they are contemporary renditions of stone water basins found in the courtyards of Joseon-period *hanok*. Water-filled *mulhwak* were placed outside the *sarangchae*, an area designated for the master of the house, to reflect the sky and to collect falling leaves to inspire poetic thought. The Joseon shapes were influenced by stone mortars dating back to the Three Kingdoms Period (37 BC–AD 668), whereas the artist sculpted these modern L-shaped pieces from old granite stone for containing water, grass, or moss.

Above One of the architect's signature design features is a water garden. Although he believes in employing indigenous materials, this pond, being in an urban environment, was filled with polished black river stones. Reclaimed column foundations form innovative stepping stones. The simple pond showcases water lilies that bloom all summer long. Wires are strung as a safety measure for visiting children playing in the upper garden.

mountain atelier

ARCHITECT HAN VAN DER STAP

Nestled in a thick pine forest 55 kilometers southeast of Seoul in the Yangpyeong area, this country retreat and studio belongs to a writer-artist couple who divide their time between here and their city apartment. Far from the hectic pace of the city, it is a place for them to work productively in a tranquil and relaxed environment. The couple bought the lot after discovering that the forest behind was a government-protected area for growing ginseng and shiitake mushrooms and thus would not be built upon. They then commissioned Dutch architect Han van der Stap to design a house which accommodated their work needs yet set up a dialogue with the stunning forest setting and the sweeping vistas of the neighboring Daebu Mountains.

Although the house is organized in free-flowing spaces, beginning with a buffered zone on the north side and moving to progressively more open expanses on the south side, the architecture was primarily governed by the artist wife's studio, which required high ceilings and generous walls. "We requested spatial continuity, functional work spaces, adequate storage for canvases and books, and easy access to the garden for a casual mountain lifestyle. Not only were our requests perfectly met, but we also couldn't be happier with this house. The success is due to the luxury of working with an architect who is also a personal friend."

The artist's studio occupies the home's largest area while the writer's study is located on the second floor of the adjacent living room, connected by a lighter-than-air arced staircase. The living room flows seamlessly into an open-plan kitchen and out to a wooden deck. Expansive glass doors lead to the garden, deck, and driveway, opening the rooms to both natural light and splendid views. All surfaces of the house are finished in white, including the high-gloss urethane-based painted floors, a "canvas" deliberately left blank to showcase works of art and an eclectic mix of antiques and inspirational artifacts.

Landscape architect and neighbor Ryu Gwang-woon repositioned some of the beautiful rock outcrops, indigenous to Korean mountains but rarely found intact nowadays, to make a dynamic spring-fed pond, and also created a trail, bordered with plantings of moss and wild flowers, that meanders through the steep-sloped forest beyond.

Left Two acrylic light sculptures, works of the artist in her signature dot pattern, flank a pair of colossal sliding doors; Ingo Maurer's Mozzkito lamp sits on one of them. The doors divide the studio and living area, creating a quiet space when concentration is needed for work. The focus of the living room is a minimal brushed stainless steel fireplace surrounded by an eclectic assemblage of art and found objects. Reminiscent of driftwood, an old rice cake board, rescued from the streets and fitted with rollers, forms an original coffee table, in rustic contrast to the sleek silk lounging cushions. The glass walls and the deck wrapping the south side of the living room capture breathtaking forest views. Alfresco dining on the wooden deck with garden-grown vegetables is one of summer's great pleasures.

Left Old carpenter's tools form a beautiful still life against a carved openwork panel on the side of an old bookshelf. This popular motif, developed in the Joseon Dynasty, is commonly found on household objects such as dishware and door handles.

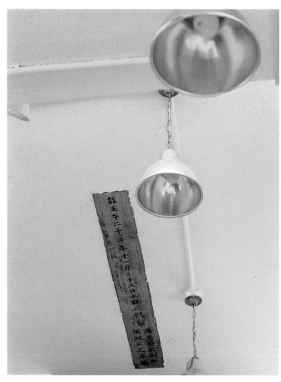

Left The writer's calligraphic work on traditional paper shows the date of the roof-raising ceremony and old phrases bestowing good fortune on the house and family. Customarily placed on the roof beam and concealed, it is here exposed on the studio ceiling for amusement. Large industrial fixtures provide additional light on dull days and in the evenings.

Left A collection of red lacquer spools and wooden tops creates another beautiful still-life image. The artist describes her work as "reviving the lives of discarded objects through creative thought." The objects filling the house, collected over many years, are deeply personal and an inspiration for her work.

Above Towering bookshelves in the light-filled studio have an almost sculptural feel about them. Housing the couple's extensive book collection, they free the floor and walls for work on large-scale canvases. The dramatic arced staircase seen in the background leads to the writer's study. Supported by a single aluminum pipe, it is designed to be practical yet visually unobtrusive.

Left The stark white master bedroom is a perfect setting for two gorgeous lacquered cabinets embellished with mother-of-pearl inlay – ornamental heirlooms from the artist's mother. A bright red sculpture created by the couple's daughter makes a strong statement in the window niche. A door leads to the wooden deck, which extends from the living room and stretches out into the pine trees.

Below left and right Two doors flank a stunning heirloom display cabinet and matching letterbox (see detail) with a finely rendered peony motif, one door leading to the entrance hall and the other to the master bedroom. Feminine and ornamental *najeonchilgi* (mother-of-pearl inlaid lacquerware) was often found in the women's quarters of traditional aristocratic residences, in contrast to the simple, natural, wood-grained furniture of the men's quarters. Confucian doctrine embraced a complex system of social conduct, with separate living quarters for men and women.

Above right A long-held dream of bathing among trees in the morning sun is satisfied by the sparkling white bathroom, its tile work mimicking the style of French artist Jean-Pierre Raynaud. The double-sink vanity counter of black Corian is shaped in whimsical curves. On the counter, an antique *jwagyeong* mirror box, an essential accouterment of a lady's room in the Joseon period, adds an interesting touch. Designed with a swivel mirror for the convenience of a lady sitting on the floor, the lower section has a drawer for storing cosmetics, combs, and hairpins. Concealed in the niche behind the tub, a glass door provides ventilation and access to the wooden deck.

Right Works in progress based on a Buddhist sutra hang in the light-filled studio. A set of steps, innovatively designed with rollers to provide access for working on large-scale works as well as seating in the studio, leads to a small bamboo garden, a space for contemplation and repose according to the vernacular of a literati-scholar's house.

traditional couturier's salon

ARCHITECT **MINN SOHN JOO**

Above Standing sentinel at the entrance to the salon is a pair of mid-Joseon Dynasty (AD 1392–1910) Korean *dong-jaseok* stone figures, originally tomb guardians (see pages 158–9), topped by two elegantly spiraled century-old iron Chinese lantern hangers.

Opposite Antique latticed Korean doors open to the *sarangbang*, a room for greeting guests by the master of a typical Joseon literati-scholar's house, that Kim has re-created for client fittings and as a showroom for displaying his bedding designs and antique furnishings. A legendary scene of nine valleys in ancient China is immortalized in a brush-and-ink painting on an old paper-and-silk Korean screen at the back of the room.

Although traditional Korean dress, or *hanbok*, is no longer worn on a daily basis, it is still the clothing of choice for special occasions, such as weddings and birthdays. In his tiny but elegant salon in the historic Sogyeok-dong neighborhood of Seoul, which also boasts an old palace, art galleries, antique shops, and the blue roof-tiled presidential residence popularly known as "The Blue House," *hanbok* designer Kim Young-seok caters to a fashionable and affluent clientele. Five years ago, with the help of architect Minn Sohn Joo, his shop, a small white cube with a Korean-style tiled roof, was transformed from an ordinary single-story house into an intimate yet functional space for artful displays of antique furnishings, traditional dress, and accessories. Here, Kim and his two assistants greet clients for consultations and fittings.

The shop's only exterior decoration is a large show window, which allows free rein to Kim's imagination through the seasons. Because of the limited space inside, priority has been given to the storage of fabrics and the many accessories that accompany the *hanbok*. In contrast to typical *hanbok* shops in which all the fabrics are displayed from wall to wall, the key design element here is compartmentalized space, which hides fabrics from view. Behind the central axis of the designer's table and showroom are other hidden areas: a dressing room, restroom, and kitchen. On display are antique furnishings and crafts for sale, most of which Kim has lovingly restored.

Committed to upholding the traditional culture and arts and crafts of Korea, the couturier studied under Koo Hae-ja, daughter-in-law of a renowned National Living Treasure who made bedding for the royal family. His apprenticeship led to the making of *hanbok*, which he decided to make more fashionable for contemporary tastes. In his versions, he retains the traditional features of the costume, such as the emphasis on the beauty of color schemes and the coordination of the different pieces – the skirt and bolero-like top should always be in different but complementary colors – but introduces new and modern color combinations. The proper way to wear and accessorize a *hanbok* is also presented in the salon. Invited to participate in the 2004 Paris collections, Kim's designs are quickly gaining international recognition.

Another goal is to encourage the use of traditional accessories with current fashion. Kim searches for and restores antique brooches, hairpins, and tiaras, and re-creates handbags according to original designs. Such exquisite handcraft of the past, made by devoted artisans for the aristocracy and royalty, is a continuous source of inspiration for the couturier's work.

The couturier has also tastefully combined Korean and more accessible Chinese antiques to furnish his salon and these are also for sale. It is extremely rare to find artifacts dating back more than 150 years since traditionally a person's belongings were burned to chase away any lingering unfriendly spirits when he passed away. Moreover, many Korean antiques did not survive the 35-year Japanese colonization and, later, the Korean War (1950–3).

Above left Adorning the wall in the waiting area are brightly glazed terracotta wall vases from China, ranging in age from 120 to 160 years. The wooden bench has been cleverly crafted from an old wooden Chinese horse feed trough.

Above Under a Korean scroll hanger, a Chinese stone Buddha dating back to the seventeenth century sits serenely in a corner of the salon near the lattice doors leading to the *sarangbang*.

Left A pair of *heukae* – Joseon-period shoes worn by civil and military officials – is placed at the entrance to the *sarangbang*. Although they were traditionally made of black leather or black cotton flannel, Kim had the ones here fabricated in suede.

Right The handsome bookcase at the back of the shop is a modern-day reproduction designed by Kim using old persimmon tree wood reclaimed from a demolished house. Propped against the wall is a framed *doturak daenggi*. This long ribbon is a reproduction of a late Joseon-period headdress worn among the gentry or by a bride for a wedding ceremony held in the royal court. The original peach-shaped orpiment stone (not shown), believed to have powers to ward off poisonous snakes and evil spirits, and peony-carved amber ornaments framed in knotted silk threads adorn the ribbon re-created in the traditional design. Custom-made stools from reclaimed jujube tree wood are grouped around an antique Chinese mahjong table.

Left A precious pair of delicately embroidered lady's *kkotshin* flower shoes from the late Joseon period takes pride of place on a stone "ironing" block. Only the gentry were allowed to wear these silk or leather shoes for weddings, ancestral rites, or special holidays. *Kkotshin* are mostly embroidered with plum blossoms, peonies, or the ten symbols of longevity. Phoenixes symbolizing royalty and high rank grace the pair shown here.

Left An ancient Tibetan Buddhist folded scripture atop a nineteenth-century Japanese chest is an exquisite stage for various accessory displays, as shown on page 98, top left.

Left Displayed on the wall is Kim's meticulous reproduction of a *wonsam* dress ca. 1680 worn by Yi Dan Ha, wife of the king's brother. This type of dress from the mid-Joseon period was also worn as everyday wear by a princess, as an official outfit for a high-ranking woman when paying a visit to the royal court, and by the queen's court attendants. The embroidery adorning the front panel denoted the status of the wearer. Although originally embroidered in gold threads, the patterns seen on the shoulder and sleeves here are stamped with gold leaf. *Wonsam* were worn with *oyo-mori*, a large braided chignon hairstyle held in place with many long hairpins.

Above An assortment of Korean ladies' hairpin cases, ranging in age from 60 to 200 years, makes an interesting display and provides excellent storage for small items.

Left These black silk satin tiaras are called *jokduri*. *Hwagwan*, seen in the center, was the most elaborately decorated with a minimum of five different stones. This particular one has antique pieces of green and yellow jade, agate, coral, pearl, and amber. The small hornlike decorations were made of coiled gold or silver wires, mostly of cloisonné, which bounce with the slightest of head movements, making the tiaras all the more exotic. Kim reproduced those on this *hwagwan* with flower-shaped brass parts painstakingly pasted with blue Chinese kingfisher feathers.

Left An exquisitely crafted three-jewel *norigae* brooch is a stunning composition of colors and shapes. The carved jade brooch is enhanced with three knotted silk tassels and charms: a pair of jade butterflies embellished with pearls, carved amber, and a piece of coral. This type of luxurious *norigae* was attached to a *dangui* jacket, which was tradition-ally worn over an aristocratic lady's bolero-like top and skirt when receiving guests or going out. Her hands would be concealed beneath the large front flap, in accordance with Confucian etiquette.

Left The couturier is also known for his exquisite bedding and tableware. Seen here is an array of heavy cotton-filled winter bedding fabricated in jewel-toned silk satins, brocades, and twill, which are either embroidered or hand sewn in patchwork. Light summer bedding is made with sheer pastel-toned Korean *moshi* linens dyed with natural plant dyes.

Top Shaded by a gnarled pine tree, a pair of 300-year-old stone tigers from southern China, wearing bemused expressions, guards the shop.

Above The *jokduri* tiara – embellished with old coral and jade beads, and five silk tassels – was also worn with the *wonsam* dress but with a flat, center-parted hairstyle, or the wedding dress called *hwalot*. Red spots were applied to the bride's cheeks with *yeonji* cosmetic, a vermilion flower pigment mixed with sable fat or wax.

Top Placed against a wall, a 350-year-old stone pedestal, originally from southern China but purchased in Thailand, is used for displaying a pair of Chinese jade lovebirds carved in Korea.

Above The show window displays Kim's imaginative re-creation of a typical scene on a Joseon scholar's folding screen, with stacked antique book-shelves and an assortment of accouterments, including brushes and inkstones. Also included is a Joseon-period *jobawi*, a girl's outing hat.

house of voids

ARCHITECT **SEUNG H-SANG**

Above An old papered latticed screen door hung horizontally over the window in the master bedroom allows soft, diffused light to enter the room.

Opposite Seen from the main corridor, which runs from the entrance to the separate tea-house, the infinity-edge water void continues to enthrall the owners and their guests with its reflections of the sky, moon, and stars. Here, it reflects the intense blue of a cloudless, mid-summer sky. The concrete block stepping stones appear to lead to the sky and beyond.

"Subaekdang," meaning "a house guarding the color white," is located 30 kilometers from Seoul in an area known as Yangpyeong. After visiting the forested site, architect Seung H-Sang decided to adopt the name "Subaekdang" after an historical house on the outskirts of Daegu City. Its alternative literary name – "guardian of voids" – also expresses the mental spirit that Korean scholars universally strove to achieve. When the architect suggested "Subaekdang" to the owners, a former prosecutor and his artist wife, he learned that the husband's traditional name (the Chinese practice of traditional names had become widespread amongst the literati-scholars in Korea by the Joseon period, 1392–1910) was Hyeon-cho, meaning "an old gentleman in the country," a fitting name for the owner of House of Voids who had plans to retire there.

The unevenly sloping site was backed by a forested hill on the north and open to distant views of the North Han River, Jungmi Mountain, and neighboring towns on the south, recalling scenes of a Pieter Breugel (1525–69) painting on a sunny day. Much to his dismay, the architect, who looks upon boundary walls as direct expressions of how the occupants of a building intend to co-exist with their neighbors and surroundings, found that the extensive landscaping needed to level the site for a home and garden required building a large retaining wall at the foot of the hill. It thus became his primary task to incorporate this element into the overall design. The resulting wall, measuring 30 by 15 meters, became the frame of the house itself. With a total floor area of 200 square meters, including the basement, the two-story building is composed of twelve voids: five interior voids and seven exterior. Whether they are covered with a roof or not, the architect's concept is that each void is an independent world, forming a boundary to the next one but never subordinate to it. The covered voids house the dining room and kitchen, master bedroom suite, living room, and teahouse on the ground floor and a single guest room on the upper floor. The other seven voids – "rooms" open to the sky – are filled with water, earth, and pebbles, or decked with stained pinewood.

Both the exterior and interior surfaces of the house are finished in white to literally express the name of the house, at the same time forming a canvas on which the occupants can fill in details to reflect their lifestyle and personalities. The architect believes that a house should be perceived as a form of life rather than an architectural structure, and that the "building" of a house begins only when the construction is complete. An important concept in Korean vernacular architecture is that a structure should not be an object in itself but a framework or vehicle, a means by which one can communicate and achieve harmony with nature. This concept is well illustrated in Masterpiece of Confucian Architecture (page 204).

Above Large windows surround the south and west corners of the living room. A granite "ironing" block, fondly referred to as "Marilyn Monroe" by the artist wife, has pride of place in a corner facing the stained pinewood deck.

Left In a corner of the traditionally appointed paper-floored master bedroom, a Joseon-period bamboo chest of drawers (*jang*) for storing books is now used to neatly organize socks, ties, and underwear. Because it grew in strong straight lines, bamboo was considered symbolic of the honest spirit of literati-scholars and was widely used for furniture in the *sarangbang* (master's room) during the Joseon period. The technique of applying split bamboo plates in geometric patterns on the surface of furniture is a craft unique to Korea and was practiced since the Goryeo Dynasty (AD 918–1392). The malleability of bamboo strips allowed for a wide range of products to be made, including brush stands, arrow holders, letter racks, and even pillows. A white porcelain *deungjan* pot for lantern oil graces the old wooden vanity chest on top of the bamboo chest of drawers.

Right An old pinewood *hamji* bowl, originally used for kneading noodle dough, mixing ingredients for *kimchi* stuffing, or storing foods, makes a novel container for CDs in the living room.

Above The platform bed in the master bedroom, made of reclaimed wood from a traditional pinewood *maru* floor, has become a popular item in recent years. Sleeping on the hard wood surface is good for the back as well as being cool on hot summer nights. Bedding is laid out every evening.

Right From a bank of low windows on the west wall of the living room, the owners and their visitors can enjoy the water void from a lower vantage point. A rice cake board surrounded by floor cushions upholstered with Korean *moshi* hemp, is used as a low table. Music entertainment is provided from Pro Arc speakers and an Audio Research system.

Left A small toilet and shower are enclosed in the towering cylindrical column in the double-height living room. Animating the tight space, light floods in through a skylight, which also affords views of the sky.

Below left The tea set in the master bedroom, by renowned ceramic artist Yoon Gwangjo, is inspired by traditional *buncheong* ware, unique in the Korean ceramic repertoire. Produced during a period of dynastic transition – the first 200 years of the Joseon Dynasty until the Japanese invasion of 1592 – *buncheong* escaped previous regulations strictly controlling artistic expression, allowing artisans to experiment freely and to adopt styles of different regions and periods. In contrast to the highly refined and stylized celadon ware, *buncheong* is endowed with rustic aesthetics expressed in incised or stamped designs and brown underglaze painting finished with a white slip glaze.

Below The 30-meter corridor extending from the entrance of the house to the papered screen door leading to the tea-house connects the various voids in the horizontal layout.

Left A pebble-filled void on the second floor provides a meditative space for creative thinking and for moon viewing. The white of the wall reinforces the effect of the simple volume framing a view of nature.

Below and overleaf The white exterior finish highlights the simple volumes containing a series of "voids" within. The largest void, a pinewood decked terrace wrapping the entire south side of the house, is framed by a steel composition that articulates the 30 by 15 meter frame of the house.

camerata music studio and residence
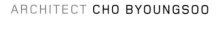
ARCHITECT **CHO BYOUNGSOO**

Above The west side of the lot is planted with white birch trees, forsythia, and mountain hydrangea interspersed with granite boulders excavated on site. Old railroad sleepers form a garden path leading to the back gate of the residence on the north side.

Opposite Ten fixed glass windows and ten open windows run along the entire south–north axis of the long, rectangular residence facing the water garden and deck. Each window is fitted with a pair of sliding doors and a screen door. The concrete column and cantilevered steps create a strong visual statement in the voluminous space. The double-height area is furnished sparingly with a pinewood dining table paired with Fritz Hansen chairs and a bookshelf made from reclaimed wood. A wide bench and coffee table made of heavy chunks of pinewood are placed at the far end of the living room. A narrow window recessed into an alcove framed in jet-black steel provides a cropped view of the Bohyun Mountain in the distance. The living room boasts a high-performance Linn audio system.

Located in Heyri Art Valley, an experimental development occupied by artists' studio-residences, galleries, and cafés 42 kilometers northwest of Seoul, this award-winning three-story 917-square meter structure made from modern-day "essentials" – exposed concrete, glass, and steel – makes a bold statement even amongst its cutting-edge neighbors in an area where contemporary architecture is mandatory.

Hwang In-yong, a well-known television and radio personality, commissioned architect Cho Byoungsoo to design the residence for himself, his wife, daughter, and photographer son, along with a music studio in which to share a 12,000 plus record collection and high-performance audio system with the public. The name of the music studio is derived from the Florentine Camerata, a group of artists, musicians, and intellectuals who convened to discuss the arts under the patronage of Count Giovanni Bardi in late Renaissance Florence. "I wanted a design in the image of a medieval European cathedral with a large, dark hall to intensify "an analog listening experience." He also asked the architect to keep the exterior simple – much like a warehouse – and for the interior spaces "to speak in spatial volumes without a trace of superficial design."

Camerata's design focuses on an increasingly popular treatment of exposed concrete cast with pine formwork, here uniquely hewn with an old bend saw, water elements, contrasts of narrow and expansive spaces, and a steel mesh screen covering the entire south façade.

The simple, box-like building is split into two volumes along a south–north axis in alignment with the direction of the hill and the open view beyond. A stone-filled water garden and a cantilevered steel staircase intersect the two volumes, the narrow slit created framing a view of the forested landscape in the distance. At the top of the stairs, a landing filled with a second water garden and a pinewood deck reached by concrete pavers, offers a different view of the distant Bohyun Mountain and the sky, this one seen through a steel mesh screen on the south side of the building, which also serves to complete the simple box-like shape. The architect describes the concrete box as being "just an envelope of space." Interior walls serve as a backdrop for the floating pinewood deck on the landing and the exterior walls for the landscape.

Top left The cantilevered steps leading to the residence on the second and third floors are built above a long channel of water filled with smooth river stones. In the afternoons, dynamic shadows are cast on the stained pine-clad exterior of the music studio.

Top As the family's lifestyle focuses on gardening – herbs and fruit specially grown for the music studio café, and for alfresco dining – the toilet and bathroom have been finished with tiles for easy hose down. The bathroom, with its deep soaking tub and stepped surrounds finished with sea foam and deep green mosaic tiles, evokes the ambience of a Moroccan *hammam* spa. A mirror is placed side by side with a window on the back wall.

Above The entire powder room, including its counter fitted with a surface-mounted porcelain sink, is covered in 5 cm-square white ceramic tiles.

Left From the top of the cantilevered stairs, concrete stepping blocks to the left pass over another stone-filled water garden to a pinewood deck from where one can enjoy a different framed view of the distant Bohyun Mountain and the sky through a steel mesh screen. This screen serves to complete the simple box shape of the second-floor landing.

Right A massive cast-concrete counter in the open-plan kitchen is equipped with two stainless steel sinks, a gas cooker top, and a dishwasher. A high-tech Zanussi ductfan, inserted flush with the countertop, elevates electronically to absorb cooking fumes.

Left The architect believes in employing indigenous materials whenever possible. Formwork for the concrete used in the building was made of pinewood planks, hewn with an old bend saw, that he spotted in a local lumberyard. The pine's rough horizontal pattern, distinctive grain, and even some splinters are imprinted into the concrete, creating a warm, handcrafted feel. The textured concrete walls have been carried through to the interior of the studio, dramatically highlighted as the sun moves across the sky through a narrow slit skylight. This penetrating shaft of light is the architect's response to the client's request for a cathedral-like structure to add a "spiritual dimension" to the music experience.

Above Suspended from the ceiling by twelve 22 mm-thick steel cables, each with a weight tolerance of two tons, a sculptural pinewood platform houses additional seating. The platform, made of slats 20 mm thick and 40 mm wide held together with wires tightened by turn buckles, is surrounded by a transparent glass railing and sandblasted glass catwalk. The platform is accessed via stairs behind the speaker wall of the music room. It also has an independent entryway from the sloped garden on the second level in response to the owner's future plans for converting it into a guest room.

Right A captivating bird's-eye view of the main 10-meter-high music hall from the floating platform reveals the symmetrical, cathedral-like layout of the furniture.

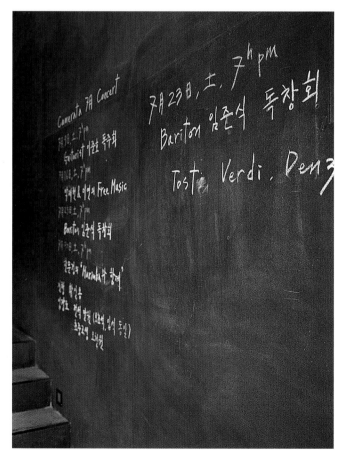

Opposite The simple, box-like building is split into two volumes along a south–north axis following the direction of the hill and the open view. A water garden and cantilevered steel staircase are installed between the two volumes. An expansive steel mesh screen covers the south façade of the building, completing the simple box shape that the architect refers to as "just an envelope of space."

Above left and left Brief bulletins concerning weekly performances are handwritten in chalk on the great Corten steel wall above the steps leading to the music studio. The cantilevered steps leading to the residence from the open garage at left are visible in the narrow slit separating the residential and music studio sections in the box-like structure.

Above Each table in the music studio, designed by the architect in solid pinewood planks and steel, is nostalgically furnished with a pencil sharpener and a pencil anchored to a river stone with a piece of string. Visitors are free to write down their requests, make notes on the music, or simply scribble on the paper. The entrance fee allows them to stay for as long as they like with the added bonus of free refills of coffee and tea brewed with homegrown herbs.

folding screen mountain retreat

DESIGNER **KIM CHOON**

Above A window in the mezzanine of the main building, which houses the designer's workspace accessed by an exterior staircase, was kept deliberately small to capture a framed view of the old Confucian school surrounded by autumn foliage.

Opposite Simply landscaped with a carpet of Goryeo grass, two iconic pine trees, and a grouping of slender maple trees, the front garden, retained by a low galvanized aluminum fence, offers uninterrupted views of Byeong Mountain and Nakdong River. The black pinewood siding of the houses blends with the great outdoors. At the same time, the box-like shapes of the house offer something new and striking in the rural village.

Narrow paths weaving through a patchwork of brilliant green rice paddies and a winding dirt road lead to the tiny rural village of Andong located 250 kilometers from Seoul. Struck by the beauty of the landscape and the rich cultural heritage of the Andong area, interior designer Kim Choon decided to build a second home here to share with his creative director wife, pet dog, and visiting friends. The house faces magical views of Byeong Mountain and Nakdong River, with its pristine white beach, a propitious geographic site known as *myeongdang* according to Korean geomancy. Appropriately named "Folding Screen Mountain," the rock cliff has a vertical drop reminiscent of a traditional brush-and-ink painted screen displaying an ever-changing view of the seasons. The tiny village is revered as one of the most scenic spots in Korea as well as being the site of Byeongsan Seowon, a Confucian school built in 1613 (see page 204). Often referred to as the spiritual capital of Korea, the Andong area is known for its cultural development since the Silla Dynasty (57–935 BC) and as home to many *yangban* families, the aristocratic literati-scholars of the Joseon Dynasty (AD 1392–1910). The traditional houses, Confucian schools, temples, and pagodas preserved in the area testify to its flourishing architectural and literary heritage.

Reflecting the traditional layout of separate living quarters for the sexes (see page 138), the public and private domains of Kim's 350-square meter house are divided into four separate annexes. The living, dining, and kitchen areas, and a traditional tearoom are housed in the main double-height pavilion while the three bedrooms are constructed as small individual buildings on either side. A monochromatic palette was chosen for the building materials – pinewood siding covered in a black oil-based water repellent stain, black galvanized steel roofing, slate for the terraces, and black *jeonbyeokdol* brick (see page 174) for the boundary walls facing the village street – to ensure that the structures blended with the surrounding landscape. Inside, the palette dramatically shifts to a stark white. Walls are hand plastered and painted white. Ceilings follow the slope of the roof. The floor of the main building is mortar colored with a durable light gray concrete stain for easy maintenance, while the bedroom annexes have been carpeted for a cozier feel and to allow the occupants to remove their shoes. Floor heating is installed in all four buildings.

In order to exploit the views generated by the location, all interior spaces are orientated to face the mountain and river, with large picture windows along the entire southeastern walls. Interior floor levels extend out to the terraces to bring the great outdoors in. A wisteria arbor shades an alfresco dining area on the main terrace, which narrows to form exterior hallways joining the bedroom annexes located on either side of the main building.

Country life here focuses on gardening, entertaining friends with tours of nearby cultural offerings, and alfresco dining. "This area is also known for its wonderful produce – apples, grapes, watermelon, garlic, chili peppers, and the legendary Andong beef. In addition, our culinary life is enriched by kind neighbors who drop off freshly harvested vegetables and fruit, homemade bottles of pungent sesame oil, and dried hot red chili peppers." The four seasons of the Korean peninsula infuse the house with poetry and delight: winter snow fluttering on the rocky mountain spears, opulent spring cherry blossoms, early summer plums to steep in locally made *soju* (a vodka-like spirit distilled from rice) for plum wine or brown sugar for plum tea, and blazing autumn foliage followed by fragrant crops of quince and persimmon.

Left One of the designer's signature features is to incorporate a traditional teahouse into a contemporary residence. This abstracted rendition has no roof and is flanked by four lighting pillars, conjuring up the image of an ethereal stage floating in the center of the living area. All woodwork has been covered in mulberry paper as in the traditional tearoom except for the thick pine-wood slabs bordering the oil-papered *ondol* floor (see page 138). The papered doors are raised, but instead of being hooked onto eaves as in traditional architecture, they are propped on bamboo rods harvested from the garden, and suspended from the ceiling by wire cables. A monk's hat hangs on the back wall. An old Japanese iron kettle is used to boil water for tea in a Korean ceramic brazier. Pieces from the designer's collection of old "ironing" blocks, carved out of solid wood instead of stone, form innovative stepping "stones" into the tearoom.

Right Kim Ku Lim's mixed media canvas hangs above a 2000-year-old earthen vessel at one end of the living space in the main pavilion. The reclaimed Zelcova wood desk and chair were crafted by the late Japanese friend and furniture maker Kimura Jiro.

Right The dishware closet between the tearoom and kitchen is from an edition of traditional bookshelf reproductions carved with calligraphic works by the designer's father. On top, bamboo harvested from the garden and baskets from travels in Morocco and Japan add tactile and visual contrast.

Overleaf Running the entire length of the southeast wall of the main pavilion, a large window provides panoramic views of the rock cliff and river. Since the visual focus is the view – photographed here in the autumn – furnishings have been selected carefully and kept to a minimum. The dining area contains a custom-built aluminum dining table paired with Fritz Hansen chairs.

Top Normally covered on the outside with mulberry paper in the manner of traditional doors and windows, this late Joseon-period chest, originally used for storing official dress for civil servants, is purposely left bare to show its geometric form and latticework. The kitchen counter installed with a halogen cooker top is visible in the background.

Above Seen from the kitchen counter, which is composed of sandblasted glass panels set into anodized aluminum shelving, a late Joseon-period low wooden *gwae* chest with top hinges has pride of place in the entrance to the main building. Originally used for storing dishware or money, its zelkova wood grain is polished to a fine sheen in the traditional way, rubbed with a waxy paste of pulverized pine nuts. Exquisite calligraphic work by the designer's father hangs above.

Top A close-up of the dishware closet shown on page 119, placed between the tearoom and kitchen.

Above In the center of the tearoom, a collection of antique bowls (see page 57) sits on a nineteenth-century table used in ancestral rites.

Above A set of fifteen monks' begging bowls turned in solid ginko wood and finished with several coats of natural lacquer adds an interesting touch to a table. Crafted in graduated sizes to fit neatly into each other and topped with a lid, begging bowls were traditionally used for pilgrimages made in the footsteps of Buddha. The local people were expected to support the monks, who took a vow of poverty, and put what food they could spare into their bowls. A scoop of rice, braised vegetables, soup, pickles, or a flower – whatever was placed in the bowls would be the monk's nourishment. The gesture of holding a bowl molds the hands into shapes of begging, waiting, and openness.

Below On the end wall of the bedroom, a "scribble" drawing by Kim Janghee hangs above a pair of precious nineteenth-century *mungap* document chests crafted in zelcova wood. Their drawers, formerly used for storing brushes, papers, and inkstones, now provide convenient storage for guests. *Ondol* floor heating (see page 138), a unique feature of Korean architecture, became popular during the reign of King Injo (r. 1623–49). Its radiant heat greatly influenced the design of household furniture that came to be mostly constructed with legs.

Above and below left and center In one of the guest bedrooms, Korean landscape photographs by Joo Myung-duck hang above an Isamu Noguchi paper lamp and an antique *soban* table (see page 152, below) carved with a Chinese character meaning good fortune. Stacks of old wooden plates used for rice cakes are topped with an aromatic candle.

Below Facing the splendid rock cliff and river views, a Jacuzzi skirted in black slate tiles is installed in a corner of the master bedroom. A woodcut print by sculptor Joel Shapiro hangs above an old Burmese Buddha head at one end.

Top A collection of antique stone sculptures and earthenware make strong statements throughout the garden. Here, in a corner off the master bedroom annex, a mid-Joseon stone tomb guardian called *dongjaseok* (see page 159) stands proudly amongst white hydrangea bushes, hosta, and fern.

Above Drops of morning dew on lotus leaves create a quintessentially Korean image in the garden pond planted with wild water grass, lotus, and water lilies. The pond is home to a family of frogs, which provide music in the summer for a chorus of cicadas and crickets.

Right The house glows in the early evening after a refreshing summer shower. Dramatically suffused in misty clouds, the ever-changing views of the "folding screen mountain" is precisely why the designer elected to build his second home in this remote part of the country,

living with art

ARCHITECT / DESIGNER **MICHAEL McNEIL & CHUNG JAEWOONG**

Below Resin-impregnated wood panels manufactured by Prodema, selected for their water resistance, cover the largest volume of the house, while cement-fiber panels from Silbonit surface the back. Gray-tinted stucco on the remaining surfaces successfully marries the diverse materials.

Opposite Two large canvas canopies shield the exterior stairwell leading to the upper-entry level from the elements. Clear glass has been used on the balustrades to dilute any visual interruptions.

By the time a high-profile art dealer and collector decided to build her own house, she was well versed in the language of design and construction. For over twenty-two years she had worked with various architects, designers, and building contractors on the initial construction and subsequent expansions of her gallery. Since the gallery had finally taken shape to her satisfaction, she turned her attention to the private domain: a home which reflected her profession as well as provided a comfortable living space for herself, her husband, and an adult son. High ceilings were necessary for installing large pieces of art but a cold museum-like feel was to be avoided at all costs. To fulfill her desire for a casual loft-like home that was easy to maintain, she consulted Michael McNeil and Chung Jaewoong, the New York-based architect/designer team of K+C Design, who had once carried out a successful renovation and expansion of her gallery.

The owner purchased the relatively small lot in the exclusive residential area of Seongbuk-dong because of its convenient location, ten minutes from her gallery. Surrounded on all four sides by houses, a major design consideration was that the occupants be able to enjoy privacy, but at the same time the building should be in visual harmony with the neighborhood. The design team took cues from the rich earth tones of the materials in the neighboring wood-clad houses as well as the *giwa* roof tiles of historic Gyeongbokgung Palace across the street from the gallery. Resin- impregnated wood panels manufactured by Prodema, selected for their superior resistance to moisture during the rainy season, were used to cover the largest volume of the house, while cement-fiber panels from Silbonit surface the back of the house. To unify the materials, a gray-tinted stucco was applied on the remaining surfaces.

Embracing the "less is more" Miesian aesthetic, the design team embarked on the project from the perspective of gallery design and loft living. The result is an exceptional contemporary residence with a floor area of 565 square meters in which spaces flow fluidly from one to another. On the second floor, which is the entry level of the residence, the open-plan design lends itself well to the dual functions requested by the owner: as a stage for showcasing art to potential clients in a residential setting, and as a comfortable living and dining area for family and friends. The third floor, in contrast, is a much more private area, which has been discretely divided into separate rooms.

"Based on my experience as a dealer of international contemporary art in Korea, I find that many collectors still have very conservative tastes. There is a marked increase in the interest in and knowledge of contemporary art but when it comes to installing art in their homes, people still tend to be a bit hesitant. I, myself, learned about living with art from visiting my colleagues' and clients' homes in Europe and America." Indeed, being in her house proves that contemporary art is easy to live with.

Above The dining room is a blend of geometric harmony. Installed at the far end is an outstanding piece of mid-century design: the original modular wall cabinet system co-designed by Charlotte Perriand and Jean Prouvé ca. 1958–60, recognized as the most influential and innovative furniture designers of the twentieth century. The ovoid forms of the Georges Jouve flower vases add visual rhythm to the rectilinear lines. The large painting, titled "Daphne," is by Anselm Kiefer.

Left Christian Liagre's gray leather bar chairs pull up to the Carrera marble slab breakfast counter, a favorite family gathering place. The streamlined aluminum and sandblasted glass kitchen cabinetry is from the Italian company Poliform, while the appliances are from Sub-Zero, Miele, and Gaggenau.

Right and overleaf The living room is entered direct from the entrance hallway. Above the fireplace at the far end of the room is a classic Serge Mouille lamp. A small oil painting by Joan Mitchell sits on the mantelpiece while a sculpture by Louise Bourgeois is a focus of attention in the corner. On the wall between the living and dining room hangs a brilliantly hued circular "Spin" painting by Damien Hirst. The seating area is filled with an impressive collection of original mid-century American and European furniture: a Charlotte Perriand day bed, Prouvé arm-chairs, a pair of George Nakashima American black walnut coffee tables, and a Jean Royere sofa.

Left From the master bedroom, the gallery owner and her husband can enjoy a spectacular view of downtown areas. The room is appointed with a vintage bed and bench restored by Belgian designer Axel Vervoordt, Nakashima's cherry wood side tables ca. 1956, Prouvé armchairs, and an exquisite late-Joseon period *soban* tray table displaying the characteristics of those produced in the Tongyoung region of South Kyeongsang Province. In contrast to the other two major regional styles (Naju and Haeju), Tongyoung tables tend to have more elaborately designed bases. The "Blossom" chandelier by Dutchman Tord Boontje is composed of Swarovski crystals, LED lamps, and a lacquered metal branch initially created for the Swarovski Crystal Palace Project in 2002.

Right An elegant aluminum mesh screen hangs along the glass wall of the staircase connecting the public living area with the private quarters on the upper floor. The minimalist railing was finely crafted from brushed stainless steel and tempered glass by German hardware supplier/manufacturer D-line. The narrow void in between the limestone-clad treads and risers and the adjacent walls creates the illusion of a floating staircase. A LED light sculpture by Jenny Holzer adds color at the top of the landing.

Above and right The master bathroom is a sublime space sheathed in four-colored marble mosaic tiles and floored in limestone. The surface mounted marble sink fitted with brushed stainless steel KWC faucet and walnut-veneered cabinetry are both from Boffi. Deep drawers under the vanity counter provide plenty of storage for toiletries. A spacious glassed-in shower room houses a mist sauna and rain shower. A mirrored door slides open to a dressing room. In a corner niche (not shown), a Prouvé cabinet for storing toiletries sits next to a high-tech Toto toilet with motion-sensor lid.

Left A spectacular 1960s natural-edged George Nakashima walnut cabinet is placed against a wall in the master bedroom. Displayed on it is a small mobile by Alexander Calder. Above the cabinet hangs an oil painting by Gerhard Richter.

Below left The foyer is another setting for appreciating art. Visitors entering the house are greeted by a lightbox work by Jeff Wall hanging over a vintage aluminum and wood cabinet by Jean Prouvé.

Below In the white pebbled courtyard outside the dining room, *suseok* or more specifically *kyeongseok*, Korean "viewing stones" – representing condensed views of natural elements such as mountains, islands, waterfalls, and rivers – and a border of black bamboo trees add Korean essence to what is essentially a thoroughly Western residence.

Above The three-story residence, including the partially
submerged ground level housing a three-car garage and a room for
the boiler and other mechanical equipment, is built on an
east–west axis with full southern exposures. The living room is
located on the second-floor entrance level. While the uninterrupted glass wall allows stunning open views, a specially requested
overhang provides necessary shade for the valuable art inside.

Right The components of the gas fireplace in the living room (see
pages 131–3) were custom-built by US manufacturer Home Crafts.
As a contrast to the otherwise clean straight lines, the design
team chose carved MDF panels for the surround – found in Korea
and painted black on site – and a slab of natural-edged walnut for
the mantelpiece. A high tech Bang & Olufsen BeoLab 3500 speaker,
which is linked to the audio system in the third-floor family room
and remote-controlled from the living room, is mounted on the
wall above. Clean detailing and a thoroughly modern approach to
materials are evident throughout the house. The junctures of the
various materials employed are intentionally exposed to display
their texture and thickness.

hanok case study

ARCHITECT/CARPENTER **CHUNG KI-JUN**

Above The area joining the two wings of the U-shaped house is visible from the main gate across the courtyard. To the left of the gate is the modernized office wing while to the right is the traditionally appointed wing.

Opposite The *daecheong*, an intermediary space located between the private rooms, was traditionally used as a living room and for important ceremonies in the men's annex and as a work space for daily chores such as sewing and preparing food in the women's annex, although in this house the space is furnished in the style of a literati-scholar's *sarangbang* study (see page 174). Private paper-floored rooms are connected on either side of this space by partition doors, including the *anbang* (lady's room) seen on page 145. Paper-floored rooms were heated by *ondol*, a system developed in the fourth century AD, which forced smoke from wood-burning cooking stoves and exterior fire pits through flues placed under the floor and out through free-standing chimneys on the outside of the house, but the modernized *ondol* heating system utilizes an electric boiler that feeds hot water into under-floor pipes. The *daecheong* is floored with *maru*, the traditional thick pinewood flooring. Wooden-floored rooms were traditionally unheated. In this house, the *maru* parquet is used only for borders and the heated concrete section is hidden under a modern Belgian-designed paper carpet.

This charming twenty-first century reincarnation of a *hanok*, a traditional Korean house, serves as the headquarters for the Arumjigi Culture Keepers' Foundation, a non-profit cultural preservation foundation. The *hanok* is tucked away on a tiny alley in Anguk-dong, an historical area of Seoul located between two important Joseon Dynasty (AD 1392–1910) palaces, Gyeongbokgung and Changdeokgung, the latter a World Heritage Site. Because of its proximity to the palaces and its ideal *feng shui*, located as it is between the Namsan and Bukhan mountains, the area was specially allocated for the residences of aristocrats and court officials. Having escaped high-rise development, Anguk-dong remains a well-preserved area blessed with clean air and smooth traffic despite its central location. It has become a popular address for contemporary art galleries, cafes, and professional offices.

According to chairperson Hong Yun-gyun S. and advisor Chung Min-ja, "The foundation's mission is to make traditional aesthetics an integral part of contemporary life. The *hanok* serves as a working office and case study for the restoration and modernization of traditional architecture with conveniences such as electric heating, a modern kitchen and toilet facilities, glass windows, and contemporary furnishings." Originally built in the late 1950s, the *hanok* had been occupied and thoughtlessly renovated by its previous occupants. Much to the Foundation's dismay, efforts to strip the house back to its original structure proved impossible, so it was decided to rebuild from scratch using a combination of new and reclaimed building materials. The fortuitous *feng shui* of the original house, built facing west with its main entrance to the east, served as a starting point for the reconstruction.

Chung Ki-jun, a traditional carpenter commissioned to handle the reconstruction, drew up a typical vernacular plan with a U-shaped layout wrapping around a central courtyard. Confucian doctrine of the Joseon period required separate living quarters for the sexes – the women's annex called *anchae* and the men's annex called *sarangchae* – but for practical purposes, the Foundation placed all the traditional rooms in the *anchae* and the modern facilities in the *sarangchae*.

Doors and windows occupy much of the wall space in a *hanok*. Over 200 exquisite door and window panels fill the small house, testament to this unique architectural feature. The latticed windows and doors have been treated with *hanji* mulberry paper. Windows generally have a single layer of paper to allow sunlight and ventilation while partition doors between rooms have several layers of paper on both interior and exterior sides to create a seamless finish with the walls. The windows facing the exterior consist of a twin set of sliding and hinged panels to provide protection against cold and intruders.

Korean vernacular architecture was based on flexible building modules called *kan*. A unit of *kan* referred to the square area created between four posts. A ten-*kan* house meant that it had ten such spaces although the size of the squares was not always uniform. Distances between the posts were adjusted to accommodate the size requirements for each space, ranging from six (180 cm) to ten (300 cm) *cheok*. The Arumjigi house is 12 *kan* based on 7 (210 cm) *cheok*. Pinewood was almost always used for the building of a *hanok* as it was readily available and was also well suited for enduring the severe Korean climate.

Above The latticed doors of the *daecheong*, which is sandwiched between a front and back courtyard, were constructed so that they could be removed and the room left fully open to the front courtyard in summer. The minimalist *sabangtakja* shelf was a piece of uniquely male furniture used for displaying accouterments and books rather than for utilitarian purposes. Here, it is used to display Joseon-period men's hats for the Foundation's first exhibition. Intricate latticed doors on the far wall hide built-in storage for books and papers. Korean latticed doors and windows are treated with *hanji* (traditional mulberry paper) on the interior side of a room, unlike Japanese *shoji* doors that are papered on the side facing the exterior of a house. The papered latticework, crafted in a countless variety of patterns compared with the uniform grid of *shoji* doors, is also used on interior partitions, whereas in Japan it is used only in doors facing outside.

Left Stone water basins were found only in the courtyards of very wealthy households since most were purely for decoration (see page 85). This particular one was originally used in a farmer's home for cow feed.

Right The elegant curve of the pitched black *giwa* tiled roof, dormers, and deep eaves are typical features of the upper-class *hanok*. The Joseon government regulated the sizes of houses as well as the height of roofs and granite foundations according to the social status of the master of the house.

Left Boundary walls, the preserve of houses of the upper class, were constructed with stone bricks and limestone mortar joints to protect the mainly wooden structures from fire. The mortar joints were designed in a variety of geometric patterns, with red brick often being employed as a decorative accent.

Above The area joining the traditional and modern wings of the U-shaped layout connects to the *anbang*, and looks out to the courtyard and the *daecheong* beyond. Traditional sliding doors lead to the *anbang*, whereas the doors opening to the courtyard have been replaced by a large fixed-glass window in order to re-create a typical summer view from a *daecheong* when all its window panels are removed. In the traditional house, all papered latticed windows were removed in summer and stored under the deep eaves where they were suspended on large iron hooks.

Above right A *soban* tray table is laid with brass tableware crafted by master artisan Yi Bongju. This setting – for a single person – illustrates the numerous dishes that comprise a traditional Korean meal. The front gate is seen in the background.

Right Finely made latticed pinewood doors conceal a toilet in the thoroughly modern office area, complete with high-speed Internet. The floor is finished with pinewood parquet in the traditional *maru* pattern, to accommodate floor heating. Designed by architect Suh Ul-ho, the clean linear shapes of the blonde wood desks and bookshelves harmonize beautifully with the *hanok*.

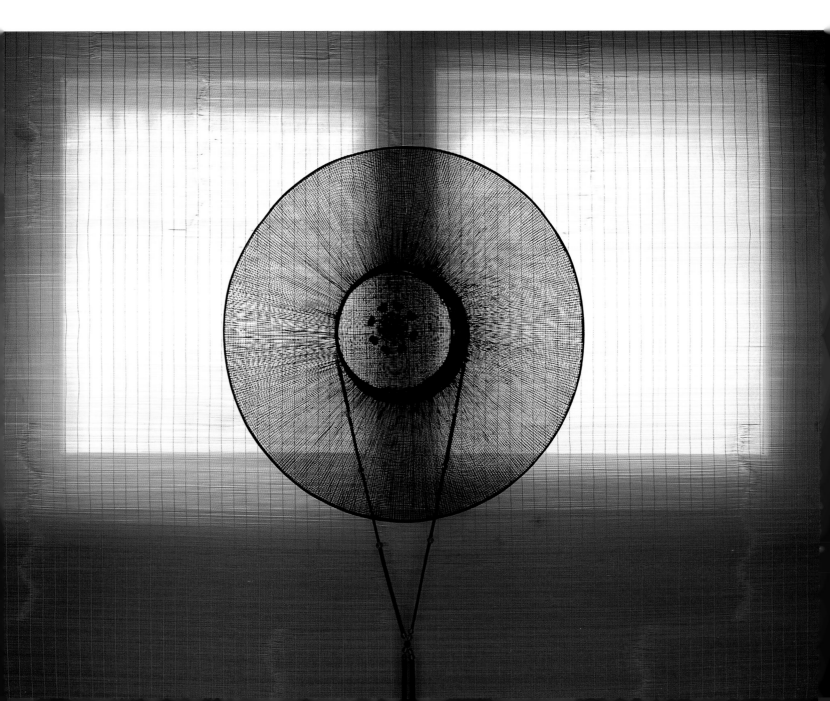

Opposite from left Crafted in oiled paper, these fashionable cone-shaped objects are traditional rain covers for hats. Actively involved in the preservation of cultural assets, the Foundation has re-created the rain hat to illustrate the form and function of traditional aesthetics.

Draped over a refined *hwoettae* clothing hanger, a silk outfit comprising a dark blue cloak, gray skirt, white bolero-like top, and small perfume sachet, makes a beautiful wall display. The cloak was worn over the head of a lady not in a palanquin, to veil her face in public, as required by Confucian doctrine.

Window and door handles are crafted in an array of materials, including forged iron rings, carved wooden knobs, and woven leather ties. Iron ring handles were used on removable door or window panels that were suspended under the eaves on large iron hooks.

Opposite below Woven from fine horsehair, an elegant hat creates a beautiful still life against a translucent papered window. The formal hat for male aristocrats in the late Goryeo (AD 935–1392) to early Joseon period can be found in a variety of shapes and sizes.

Right Displayed in the *anbang*, imbued with translucent light, the fur-trimmed Joseon-period lady's silk winter cap is designed with an open top and decorated with knots, tassels, jade, and coral beads. The latticed insets on the partition doors are papered with a single layer to let light into the room during the day and candlelight to shine out at night.

Below Traditional silk bedding and a pillow embroidered with peonies, a symbol for longevity and a happy marriage, are displayed inside the built-in cupboard. The walls of the *anbang* were treated with eight layers of *hanji* to create a smooth surface.

reflex penthouse

ARCHITECT **KIM INCHEURL**

Below A sculptural cast-concrete staircase fitted with a punched steel plate railing climbs to the fifth floor. Installed on the north side of the Reflex Building, it turns east to run across the façade at the second-floor level. The staircase recalls the famed M .C. Escher lithograph "Ascending and Descending" (1960), depicting endless stairs. Inside the five-story building is an empty shaft for installing an elevator for when the owners are no longer able to walk up the stairs to their penthouse residence.

The cutting-edge five-storied Reflex Building was designed for a building construction engineer and his wife and daughter, who requested a structure that provided rental income and flexibility in the fourth and fifth-level penthouse, allowing these two floors to be divided in the event the daughter chooses to leave home after marriage. Architect Kim Incheurl had previously designed several buildings for the family, each containing studio apartments for leasing.

Situated in what used to be a quiet, old residential area near the prestigious Ewha Women's University, one of the challenges posed by the corner lot, apart from its irregular shape, was the clashing character of the three streets facing its sides: a haphazard cityscape resulting from uncontrolled commercialization of the area where stores and restaurants catering to university students now replace old houses. There was the added irony of having to adhere to building codes specified for a residence in an area that was no longer residential. Height restrictions in Korean building codes are mandated by the width of a street facing a site as well as the distance from a new structure to the street and to the boundaries of adjacent houses. The unique trapezoidal design of the Reflex Building, with its top floors set back on a diagonal, was thus an ingenious response to the restrictions imposed by the physical and legal parameters of the site.

The building, a meticulous study in oblique angles and minimalist aesthetics, successfully addresses physical, legal, and financial restrictions as well as the client's brief by making the most of industrial materials: exposed concrete, polycarbonate, and punched steel metal. The entire south side of the 158-square meter penthouse residence is sheathed in polycarbonate panels, the architect's modern-day interpretation of traditional papered screens, which allows natural light to enter but block out unsightly views of the mixed-use area. All windows were installed on the north side facing the few remaining residential properties. Every aspect of the interior has also been designed to eliminate visual clutter: platform beds are built in, air-conditioning units are enclosed in a round steel column in the living room and in paneled bedroom walls, and all storage is concealed behind doors.

"The shape of the building was not determined by aesthetic considerations," says architect Kim. "There are times when I am trapped in a maze of legal restrictions and site conditions, and a truly unique solution presents itself." He believes that architecture merely serves as a backdrop for its occupants and their lifestyle, and should not be an object for visual appreciation nor dictate the life within. With the only request from the owners being flexibility to respond to changes in their lifestyle, he appropriately named the project "reflex," a "conditioned reaction" to given circumstances.

Right A cobalt-painted white *cheonghwa baekja* vase from the late Joseon period adds a touch of color to a corner of the living room. *Cheonghwa baekja* ware first appeared in the fifteenth century, soon becoming the preferred choice of the royal court. Special envoys were sent to China to study its technology, previously unknown to the Korean ceramic tradition of celadon ware or *buncheong* ware.

Above A streamlined modular sofa is paired with a coffee table built from reclaimed *maru*, the solid pinewood traditionally used for flooring. Sparse furnishings and polycarbonate walls contribute to a feeling of lightness and space. Although the southern orientation of a house, long favored by Koreans, has been linked to *feng shui*, this was not the architect's motivation when designing the Reflex Building. Although the traditional small-sized *hanok* had a U-shaped layout around a central courtyard, making it possible to enjoy sunlight at all times regardless of the direction it faced, in congested modern-day conditions where natural light is no longer available at all times, the architect believes that emphasis needs to be placed on the southern orientation for the purposes of energy conservation.

Above Floating above the kitchen, the glass-enclosed master bedroom is pure minimalism, its furnishings limited to an elegant top-hinged wooden *gwae* chest from the late Joseon period and a built-in pinewood platform bed. The wardrobe and other storage areas are concealed behind pinewood doors. A skin of polycarbonate on the windows ensures privacy, at the same time contributing to the simplicity and calm of the room.

Below The long cast-concrete counter, sealed with polyurethane to guard against water and grime, dominates the functional galley kitchen. Half of the counter, installed with a gas cooker top and a sink equipped with a professional-grade pre-rinse faucet which speeds cleaning up and supplies water directly to pots on the gas stove, is used for preparing meals. The other half serves as the dining table. The entire left wall, finished in floor-to-ceiling pinewood boards, houses cupboards for kitchen utensils and tableware. The door at the far left leads to a utility room.

Opposite The textured concrete walls on the outside of the building are carried into the interior. A *gwae* chest placed in front of the sloping living room wall sheathed in polycarbonate, complements the house's cutting-edge ambience. Korean furniture is noted for its sleek lines and surfaces and absence of superfluous ornamentation. Though originally designed for a traditional lifestyle of sitting on an *ondol* floor, chests like this are much-appreciated artifacts in many contemporary homes because of their timeless beauty. The kitchen counter is visible through the open stainless steel-framed pinewood door.

Right An elegant late Joseon-period *bandaji* "half-door" chest, its front panel divided and hinged to open, stands behind the sofa. Although *bandaj* were mostly built for storing larger items such as bedding and clothing, some, like this one, were made with inside shelves and drawers for holding smaller items. Zelkova wood was the popular choice because of its stunning wood grains. The pinewood door next to the chest leads to a traditional papered *ondol* guest room.

Right The most distinctive features of the building's design are its trapezoidal shape and the treatment given to its expansive exposed concrete walls. Formwork for the concrete used throughout the house was made of narrow pinewood boards. The concrete has been imprinted with a seemingly endless horizontal pattern as well as the subtle grain of the wood. As the sun moves across the sky, different planes of the concrete texture are highlighted, mimicking a gentle flow of water.

collector's hillside haven
ARCHITECT JEAN-MICHEL WILMOTTE

"Many say that the Pyeongchang-dong area is suitable only for artists and politicians, not for businessmen, because of its strong and volatile *gi* (see page 18), but I have raised a family and run a successful business here for the past twenty-five years," says the recently retired owner. Deeply impressed by the hillside chateaux owned by his Swiss partners that he often visited during his business travels, he yearned for a similar home in a hillside setting. He also gathered from his partners over the years the philosophy that a family-oriented lifestyle and an early retirement in which to pursue life-long passions constitute a successful life. Pyeongchang-dong, a residential area in the old part of the city on the northern side of the river, which enjoys views of three neighboring mountains (Bukhan, Inwang, and Bugak), proved to be an ideal location for this connoisseur of the arts and ardent gardener.

Over twenty years ago, at a time when most families in Seoul were abandoning "old-fashioned" single houses and rushing to "modern" apartments in the burgeoning Gangnam district south of the Han River, the owner, his wife, and their two young sons made the bold move from a highly desirable apartment to their first house in Pyeongchang-dong.

One day in 2000, the retired businessman received a visit from the renowned French architect Jean-Michel Wilmotte, who was in Pyeongchang-dong designing the Gana Art Center. The architect, a devotee of historical stone art and ruins, was extremely interested in the owner's extensive collection of old Korean stone sculptures. One thing led to another and before long the owner found himself accepting the architect's offer to design a new house on the same lot, which would incorporate his various collections.

Seeking ways to harmonize the building with the surrounding natural environment, the architect amalgamated it into the existing mature garden through the use of dark slate for the entryway, white limestone for the exterior, and his signature stepped wooden deck. A simple layout within the expansive 920-square meter floor area was designed to house the owner's extensive art and antique collection as well as fulfill the practical needs of the three generation family. Best known for inventing the concept of "inner architecture of cities" and his widely applauded refurbishment of the Richelieu wing of the Louvre Museum, the architect seeks to establish a style that is "discreetly contemporary" while exhibiting a great sensitivity to culture and art.

Left The Bohyeonbong peak of Bukhan Mountain, considered sacred by *feng shui* scholars, is visible in the distance. The whiteness of the Spanish limestone exterior reinforces the effect of the simple volumes that vary with light and shadow. Slits and windows create a play of solids and voids on the massive white walls.

Left The west wing, housing the master bedroom, dressing room, and bathroom, is located to the left of the central courtyard. An aluminum sculpture by Korean artist Min Gyun-hong makes a bold statement at the end of the hallway. The door on the right leads to a guest room. The 14-mm-thick oak flooring manufactured by Höns was specially imported from Germany.

Below A small, tastefully framed courtyard in the center of the residence, filled with bamboo trees and a 350-year-old stone lantern, forms the axis for movement around the house. The living room is visible behind. Korean stone lanterns, called *sukdeung*, such as the one in the courtyard, have Buddhist origins, signifying enlightenment and rebirth, and were traditionally crafted only for temples. The earliest stone lanterns originate from the Baekje Kingdom (18 BC–AD 660) but the development of their styles did not reach its pinnacle until the Unified Silla period (AD 668–935). Lighting of the lanterns at temples was to honor the Buddha as well as to provide night-time light. It was not until the Joseon period (AD 1392–1910) that such lanterns were seen adorning tombs for royalty and aristocrats. Several finely crafted, freestanding bookshelves from the late Joseon period flank the walls on both sides of the courtyard.

Right At the owner's request, the dining room was designed for enjoying expansive views of Bugak Mountain. Furnishings have been deliberately kept simple so as not to interfere with the surroundings. Lastra 8 from the Flos Collection, designed by Antonio Citterio and Oliver Low, is suspended above a glass dining table.

Left In a small sitting room in the basement level, an old rice cake board forms an unusual tea table for a pair of Campiello armchairs produced by the Italian manufacturer Zanotta. The antique wooden *gireogi* wild geese figures in the bookshelf were used in the traditional marriage ceremony (see page 188). The room invites appreciation of the works of some of Korea's modern masters: an abstract bronze sculpture of a human body in motion by Ryu In (1956–99), who was active mostly in Korea during his short life; an early painting above the bookshelf by Lee U-fan, internationally acclaimed for his minimalist brushstrokes on white canvas, and actively working in France and Japan; and to the right a painting by Lee Ungno (1904–89) from his "Letter Series" of the 1970s depicting his modern interpretation of Korean calligraphy.

Above right A staircase leads to the second-level area built for one of the owner's sons, his wife, and their children. The geometric lines of the Roy Lichtenstein lithograph on the landing echo the black steel staircase railing built framing the counter-sunk glass balustrade, which also harmonizes with the style of the custom-made windows spread throughout the residence.

Right The open bookshelf in the far corner of the owner's study showcases fine examples of white-glazed Joseon porcelain, the embodiment of Joseon-period aristocrat-scholar aesthetics: understated and humble, yet elegant and refined. A porcelain vase on the lower shelf, its flaws much coveted by connoisseurs, is re-created on canvas by hyper-realistic painter Ko Younghoon. Early Korean customs involved setting and carrying individual dining tables. Called *soban*, these tray tables are unique to Korean culture and were developed to meet the requirements of different regional cuisines and a varying number of dishes. This resulted in a fascinating range of styles: octagonal, square, rectangular, and circular, either with a single pedestal base or with two or four legs. Ginko wood was most commonly used because it was strong yet light, making the tables easy to carry. One of the tray tables here is from the Naju area, characterized by the angular lips of the corners and the straight, sturdy legs, while the other is from the Tongyoung area, which focused more on elaborate bases.

Left Landscaped by the owner, the magnificent garden is planted with pine, zelkova, juniper, and azalea trees, archetypal Korean images, to provide a backdrop for a museum-quality collection of Joseon stone figures and lanterns dating back over 200 years. During the Joseon period, decoration in houses included paintings and stone sculptures but the shapes and heights of stone pillars were regulated by the government and allowed only for the *yangban* class – members of the nine classified offices of the military and literati branches of the government.

Right Doors on either side of the windows provide access to the stepped *ipe* wood deck – the architect's signature feature and the owner's favorite sitting spot – designed to reinforce the sense of continuity between the inside and out. It is planted with a single iconic pine tree. The terrace and garden can be approached directly by a stairway from the main gate.

Right A 150-year-old stone tomb guardian greets visitors at the foot of the stairs leading to the front door. The owner was attracted to its abstract and geometric form. Called *dongjaseok*, such figures were placed in pairs facing each other in front of a tomb next to *mangjuseok*, octagonal stone pillars on pedestals usually sculpted in the form of a lotus blossom. The young boy, representing innocence, served as a trusting guide to Buddha or to *myungwang*, a Korean mountain deity.

Far right Judging by their official headdress and the batons in their hands, these stone guardians are a pair of *mungwanseok*, figures of civil officials. Stone figures of civil service officials and military officers were carved in a variety of styles and erected in front of royal tombs under the influence of Tang China in the eighth century during the Unified Silla period. The styles of these stone sculptures were simplified during the Joseon period.

photographer's hideaway

Above The view through the wooden gate shows the lush bamboo grove and the steps leading up to the two *hanok*.

Opposite Located right next to the Little Building, the two *hanok* are surrounded by a grove of brilliant green bamboo and a wall of stacked black *giwa* roof tiles, placed in such a way that they follow the steep incline of the site. Such walls are common in Korea where buildings constructed on sloped sites, especially if backed by a mountain, are considered to have ideal geomantic properties. Honed granite steps lead to a sturdy wooden gate built into the wall.

In a small four-story red brick-faced building in Gahoe-dong, an historical area of Seoul now fashionable among the design community, a photographer has carved an intimate niche out of a space measuring a mere 14 meters square. The building, appropriately named the "Little Building," was constructed in 1999 for a publisher of traditional Korean music. Roughly 40 percent of the lot comprises a steep incline of jagged rocks – a highly undesirable feature for most prospective buyers – but the music publisher thought the rocky slope was the perfect site for fulfilling his long-cherished dream of building a traditional *hanok* house, which was constructed soon after the Little Building was complete. Behind the *hanok*, but not visible from the photographer's studio, is a second, much smaller *hanok*, a mere 10 meters square, built at the same time, which the owner occasionally uses as a teahouse.

As a good friend of the owner, the photographer was involved in the design of the Little Building right from the start, and he shifted from his former studio in Gangnam on the south side of the Han River immediately after its completion. The photographer's studio, storage for his equipment, and space for his assistants are located on the top floor. The spaces on the other three floors, carved up into various sizes, are occupied by the owner's recording studio and the studios of three other friends: a book designer, graphic designer, and cinematographer. The photographer's tiny room is filled with an eclectic blend of rustic furniture, photographs, books, and bric-a-brac, all reflecting his taste for the unusual. An efficient use of the limited space is demonstrated by the inclusion of a large bookcase along one wall and CD racks and a high-end audio system (Audio Research pre-amp, Studer CD player, and McIntosh 275 power amp) placed on or next to the walls. A wine refrigerator and espresso machine make life at the workspace more enjoyable. From this small space, the photographer oversees the daily management of his studio, Apo Associates, which concentrates mostly on editorial work, and Guru Visual, a company that publishes catalogues.

The focus of the room is not on its furnishings and accouterments but on what is located outside its small confines: an elegant *hanok*, almost within arm's reach of the window! Located right next to the building, the *hanok* is surrounded by a lush bamboo grove and a traditional wall made of stacked black *giwa* roof tiles bound by a mixture of limestone, clay, and sand. Built into the wall is a small wooden gate. "There's no question that in any other situation, a neighboring building built so close to a window would be highly unpleasant but here I am blessed with the wonders of traditional architecture," enthuses the photographer.

Not long after the photographer moved in, he was able to witness the skills of carpenters employing traditional building techniques in wood. During the three months following the setting of the foundation stones, the master carpenter and his four assistants were seen doing nothing else but molding the pinewood columns to the foundation stones and sanding and carving the roof rafters, floorboards, and joinery. The columns were then erected, followed by the rafters and eaves, and finally the black *giwa* roof tiles. Six months later, the main *hanok* and the small one behind it were complete.

Right A partial view of the roof tiles, pinewood eaves, and latticed screen doors of the adjacent *hanok* is framed in a small window fitted next to a structural column. It is the larger of two houses built on the rocky-sloped site by the owner of the Little Build-ing, and is currently leased to the eminent *pansori* master Park Songhee, who has been designated a Human Cultural Asset. Originating in south-west Korea in the seventeenth cen-tury, *pansori* is a traditional art form in which a *chang* singer recites drama to the accompaniment of a drum. Its narrative musical form is unique to Korea and was proclaimed by UNESCO in 2003 as a Masterpiece of the Oral and Intangible Heritage of Humanity. A wine refrigerator sits below the window, together with a small metal filing cabinet for storing valuables. Throughout the building, which was specially designed to accommodate studios – not apartments – heating is provided by radiators instead of conventional under-floor heating.

Right Two rustic tables made from the doors of a wooden gate salvaged by the photographer from a demol-ished house in the countryside, are arranged next to each other, domin-ating the center of the small room. Doubling as the photographer's desk and a meeting table, the tables are also set with an electric kettle and utensils for serving treasured tea to visitors.

Right The original iron nails are visible on the tabletop shown below left.

Below The simple chest, a reproduction of a *sarangbang* bookshelf in a scholar's study, is used to hold wine glasses. A Faema espresso maker sits on top. Tea utensils for brewing cups of freshly harvested tea are at the ready on the table.

Top Assorted Korean ceramics organize desktop bric-a-brac.

Above On the table, tea is stored in a dark brown-glazed *onggi* pot from Jingwang, a small village in rural South Jolla Province. Also called "breathing pottery," *onggi* ware has excellent temperature and humidity control, and is thus well suited for storing the fermented ingredients that are integral to Korean cuisine. Whereas porcelain is smooth and dense, *onggi* is light and porous. Hand thrown with roughly mixed clay and kilned at low temperatures, pockets of air are trapped beneath the hardened ceramic surface allowing it to breathe and prevent stored foods from spoiling.

Top Formerly used to hold rice cakes, old square wooden dishes now frame Polaroid pictures.

Above Writing utensils are within easy reach on the *najeonchilgi* plate (see page 90), reproduced by the Ho-am Art Museum.

Above Another set of gates at the top of the steps leads to the courtyard and the first *hanok*. Affixed to the doors are paper talismans to ward off misfortune and bring blessings to the household. Such talismans have been popular for centuries and can easily be found in homes, in people's wallets and purses, and even inside pillows. Unlike Chinese talismans that were made to ward off ghosts, Korean talismans are unique in their attempts to appease ghosts and to harmonize with such spirits.

Left The photographer recalls one rainy evening in his office: "The sound of raindrops falling from the eaves of the *hanok* melded with the distant strumming of a *gayageum* (a traditional Korean harp with twelve strings). Coupled with the amber-toned light softly glowing through the papered windows, it was a scene too perfect for words."

bedrock manor

ARCHITECT **KIM KAI CHUN**

Above The view of the residence from the south illustrates how it is positioned right up against the huge bedrock. The carefully studied placement of windows crops lovely views of Bukhan Mountain in the distance and the grove of pine trees surrounding the house.

Opposite The majestic entrance leading to the residence, elevated high above the level of the street, is composed of a sequence of steps and landings paved in granite. The sharp minimalist surfaces of the house are softened by the roughly hewn fieldstone retaining walls and lush plantings of white birch trees, peonies, azaleas, and cosmos flowers.

With their children about to go abroad for studies, a successful businessman and his wife decided to leave their old home in Gangnam, an increasingly congested area on the south side of the Han River, and seek solitude in a more peaceful part of the city. "I looked at so many sites for building our dream home," recalls the wife, "including places outside the city limits. But in 1999 my search ended here, in Pyeongchang-dong, where I encountered a house for sale in this breathtaking location. The scenery instantly reminded me of Wuthering Heights." Having rejected design proposals from two architects, the owners attempted to renovate the existing house with the help of an interior designer but were unhappy with the progress. Thus, in 2001 architect Kim Kai Chun was called upon. The architect recalls seeing what was basically a construction site with renovations halted halfway. Because the modified structural frame was clearly unsafe, he strongly recommended rebuilding from scratch. His design proposal immediately won the hearts of the entire family.

Visiting the 2100-square meter site on a late autumn day, the architect, who has a background in Asian philosophy, including *feng shui*, was struck by the presence of particularly strong winds on the pine-clad rocky pinnacle that sloped steeply on four sides. For the sake of the family's future happiness, health, and prosperity, he felt it best to take this central rock and pine grove as a starting point for his design. The decision was taken to modify the steep incline and open the site to the wondrous views of Bukhan Mountain. The first three months of construction were thus spent excavating dirt and rock in order to lower the entire level of the land by one meter. When a huge rock was uncovered beneath the exposed pinnacle, it was decided that the house would be placed right up against it. Several months were also spent selecting the gray limestone for the exterior, which blends perfectly with the mountainous surroundings. The resulting residence stands in complete harmony with nature, at the same time acting as a vehicle to make nature more approachable.

A majestic entranceway built with a cascade of granite-paved steps and landings leads to the second-floor entry level of the three-story 328-square meter residence towering above the street. Inside, no obvious boundaries, such as corridors – which the architect believes are a wasted use of space – break up the space. The free-flowing areas are finished in subdued creamy white and gray materials, selected for their harmony and hues rather than their individual qualities. The walls are swathed in *hanji* (traditional mulberry paper) and limestone, the latter continuing in from the exterior, both non-reflective materials chosen to absorb light. Floors in the public areas are in light-toned Crema Marfil marble, while the transitional spaces are covered in walnut wood parquet. The entry (second) level contains the living room, traditional tearoom, dining and kitchen areas, powder room, and master bedroom suite. On the upper level are three bedroom suites for the couple's two children and for guests, and a family room – the entertainment hub of the house – equipped with high-end McIntosh amp and disk player, JMlab speakers, and a piano. The family room and transitional areas are finished in walnut wood parquet while the bedrooms have been surfaced with a Scandinavian woodchip material that looks and feels very much like traditional oil-papered floor but is more resistant to wear and tear. A long ipe wood deck runs along the entire south side of this upper level, connecting to the family room, water garden, and son's bedroom. The bedroom suites for the daughter and guests on the north side of the house have private terraces. The garage, storage area, housekeeper's room, and study are housed in the lowest, partially submerged level.

Once inside the house, the carefully planned orientation of the rooms and placement of windows allow such spectacular views of the natural environment that one easily forgets that this residence is located in the midst of a sprawling metropolis.

Above The granite peaks of Bukhan Mountain along with the pine trees, boulders, marigolds, and chrysanthemums in the garden make a perfect picture from the dining room. The Fino frosted glass dining table and denim-upholstered chairs are designed by Holger Janke for German company Cor. A contemporary lighting fixture made from a folded sheet of stainless steel is suspended above. The edge of the large bedrock is visible on the south side.

Right from top: An alfresco dining area jutting over the south, steep-faced cliff was designed by the owners, and is a favorite spot to sit and admire the daily harvest. The vegetable patches, located in the lower south side of the spacious grounds, are filled with carrots, spinach, radish, scallions, Korean cabbage, pumpkin, and garlic chives. The annual *kimjang kimchi* is made with homegrown vegetables. The architect was entrusted with all design decisions pertaining to the building whereas the owners, both avid gardeners, decided to design the garden themselves with fieldstone retaining walls, vegetable patches, alfresco dining areas, and railroad sleeper steps that follow the steep gradient of the site.

Left The architect deliberately positioned the living room to face the best views of the site: the huge bedrock and a grove of pine trees. A comfortable grouping of black leather Arthe sofas and armchairs designed by Wulf Schneider for Cor fill the room. A small oil on canvas by Yi Chungji depicting a Korean chimney top and mixed media on wood by Han Jung-hee hang on the walls. A pair of late Joseon-period storage chests sits in front of the tall windows that extend to the upper level, a special request from the owners. Constructed to bridge the lower-level voids, the family room looks down on the living room. The open plan allows the presence of other family members as well as the sound of the piano to be felt and heard throughout the house.

Left and right Located off the living room, a contemporary tearoom is furnished with a modern ink painting by Kim Chun-ok and exquisite antiques. The painting hangs above a late Joseon-period (1392–1910) chest with elaborate hardware. Called *sung sunggi bandaji* for the many holes in its cast-iron ornaments, and made of linden wood, such chests came originally from the coastal Bakcheon area of Pyeongan Province. A late nineteenth-century white porcelain pedestal dish used for ancestral rites is set atop together with a pair of early Joseon-period iron candlestands from a Buddhist monastery. The rare wooden oil lamp stand, also from the same period, is an ingenious design with adjustable arms. Natural oils were poured into its ceramic dish. A decorative lacquered *hwa-hyeong* (flower-shaped) *soban* table of ginkgo wood, originating in Gyeonggi Province, is painted with a circle motif. The pinewood tea table is formed of an old rice cake board. The limed oak wood sliding doors with latticed insets purposely left exposed, are the architect's contemporary rendition of traditional Korean doors.

Left A large roof deck clad in ipe wood was built to enjoy panoramic views of the Bukhan Mountain to the north and the sprawling metropolis to the south. It also provides ample space for sunbathing and for drying vegetables and chili peppers, important staples of Korean cuisine. A water garden installed on the third floor (not shown) below the roof deck, is filled with a graphic composition of granite chunks and water hyacinths.

Below left Details of the items in the tearoom shown on pages 170–1: the decorative lacquered *hwa-hyeong* (flower-shaped) gingko *soban* table; the pair of early Joseon-period iron candlestands; and the elaborate hardware on the late Joseon-period *sung sunggi bandaji* chest.

Above right The natural pine grove embracing the daughter's bedroom evokes memories of a child's tree house. Appointed with contemporary silk bedding quilted in a traditional pattern, the leather-upholstered bed made by German manufacturer Interlübke is flanked by anodized aluminum side tables. Light for reading comes from aluminum-encased sconces at each end. Two late Joseon-period tobacco cases on the bedside table are now used to store accessories. An exquisite antique bamboo *juk-buin* ("bamboo wife"), used to wrap one body's around on hot summer evenings, rests on the bed.

Right The walls of the son's bathroom are sheathed in glass mosaic tiles. Found in different colors throughout the bathrooms, the tiles are in response to the wife's request for a little more color to offset the subdued palette of the residence. Marble surfacing skirts the American Standard tub fitted with a shower mixer from Grohe. The marble vanity counter, supported on stainless steel panels, is fitted with a surface-mounted porcelain sink and faucet from German manufacturer Kludi.

maestro's utopian vision

ARCHITECT KIM SWOO-GEUN & SPACE GROUP

Born in Seoul in 1931, the late Kim Swoo-geun is highly esteemed for his contribution to the development of contemporary Korean architecture. After receiving his MA from the University of Tokyo, the 30-year-old Kim returned to Korea in 1961. Over the next twenty-five years, he designed 230 works, including planned and competition projects, and executed over 150 of them. He passed away in 1986 at the early age of 55. Kim's dynamic architectural style, a composite of Korea's traditional spirit and modern culture, has attracted attention all over the world for its humanistic and organic qualities.

Recognized as one of Kim's major works, along with the Kyeongdong Presbyterian Church (1982) and the main stadium for the 1988 Seoul Olympic Games, the Space Building, designed for his practice of the same name, overlooks the magnificent grounds of the Biwon, the Secret Garden of the Joseon Dynasty (1392–1910) Changdeokgung Palace. The original building was erected in 1971, followed by the construction of a secondary annex off the reception area. Finished with *jeonbyeokdol* carbonized bricks, the two five-story structures have a combined floor area of 1350 square meters. By applying the vernacular of "human scale," Kim designed an organic flow of internal spaces: small and large, high and low, open and closed, dark and light. The building is Kim's masterpiece, embodying all aspects of his ideology. To this day, his free-spirited legacy lives on in the relaxed studio atmosphere, where staff members are visible throughout the buildings discussing projects in any available space, whether large or small, closed or open, and even on the benches outside.

Abstractions of traditional aesthetics are manifest throughout the building. The brick façade is a sculptural composition in which bricks are laid at right angles so that they protrude at various points, with some cut in half to create further irregularities. The textural treatment of the brick surface expresses the aestheticism of Korean materiality, in which the beauty of handcraft and natural materials are an integral part. Upon visiting the building, many foreign architects have commented that it is not only a representation of Korean vernacular architecture, but also of its topography. Mountains, oceans, valleys, and fields are all present in the maze of spaces.

The architect is also well known for his insight into "Korean Space" and cherished intermediary spaces called *gan*, which allow for spontaneous happenings and play. For Kim, the expression *meot*, loosely translated as "a sophisticated form of cultural panache," best defined this kind of leisurely time and space. He found the essence of *meot* in the traditional *madang*, *sarangbang*, and *daecheong*. The *madang* or courtyard is positioned to connect to each room in the traditional house. Although it is an exterior space, it functions as an interior space when used in combination with the *daecheong* (see page 138). The *sarangbang*, the master's study, referred to as the "Ultimate Space" by the architect, was a space for intellectual pursuit and creative activity, such as writing and painting.

As an avid patron of the arts, Kim established a magazine, gallery, and performance space. He also generated a re-evaluation of traditional art forms and introduced avant-garde culture into the mainstream. People from diverse fields constantly circled around the architect, contributing to his reputation as the "maestro of architecture and culture." Kim strongly believed that it was an architect's moral obligation to provide familiar and friendly elements in a space. He visualized architecture as being pliant instead of rigid and enclosed, yielding to its inhabitants as well as to the environs. Coining this concept as "Negativism for Architecture," he often quoted lines from a Robert Frost poem called "Mending Wall" to express his sentiments: "Before I built a wall I'd ask to know What I was walling in or walling out, And to whom I was like to give offence. Something there is that doesn't love a wall, That wants it down."

Previous page Reminiscent of the multifunctional *daecheong*, the second floor of the original building has an open plan. The reception and waiting area flows into a conference room, stairwell, and the late maestro's office located on a skip a floor above. The brick-walled reception area faces an uninterrupted glass wall connecting the exterior and interior spaces, as in a traditional *daecheong*. An imposing earthenware vessel from the Three Kingdoms period (37 BC–AD 668) and an elaborate *jang* chest from the late Joseon period (1392–1910) make bold vernacular statements at the entrance.

Above Every detail of the maestro's office has been preserved as a memorial museum, open to the public by appointment. His beloved 1970s plastic stationary items occupy the surprisingly modest desk, a pine board supported by two book-filled cubes. The watercolor drawing is by the architect himself and the photograph is of the Masan Yangdeok Cathedral, one of his acclaimed projects.

Left and right Bookshelves lining the wall of the conference area on the reception floor are filled with vintage books – AIA technical manuals, books on Korean arts and culture, and Japanese architectural books – and an architectural model submitted to the International Competition for the Paris Pompidou Center in 1969, won by Richard Rogers and Renzo Piano.

Above left A detail often seen in the late architect's work, which expressed his view of Korean humanism, is the use of stepped square wooden columns, here at the entrance of the annex building. Instead of employing a single, definitive line that Kim considered more characteristic of Western nature, he preferred to graduate lines, dividing them into smaller units.

Above center A round *dwiju* grain chest, on which stands a bronze sculpture, nestles against the papered brick wall in a corner of the architect's office. Its round shape is unique to Gangwon Province. Although wood was abundant, woodworking skills remained undeveloped in this area, isolated as it was from the rest of the country by the Taebaek Mountains, so it was common for the people to make these primitive vessels out of tree trunks.

Above right A bird's-eye view of the stairwell in the annex building. Windows have been placed at each level for natural light to enter during the day. The widths of the steps are graduated, becoming narrower as they ascend to the top landing, which leads to a roof deck.

Below The Glass Forum, a five-story 479-square meter building with a basement, was added in 1997. Conceived in the spirit of the maestro by his successor, the late Jang Seyang, it was deliberately designed as a transparent structure so as not to obstruct views of the Secret Garden and the original buildings. It houses additional work spaces and a large presentation room filled with architectural models of the practice that now employs over 200 staff members. The roof of the *hanok* built in the courtyard is visible below.

Right The granite-paved *madang* courtyard, accessed through the exterior foyer or via stairs from the old building, is home to a magnificent stone pagoda from the late Joseon period and a restored *hanok*. The *hanok*, which has stood in the courtyard for decades, initially belonged to the Hyundai conglomerate but was acquired by the Space Group upon the death of Hyundai's founder in the late 1990s. In 2003, it was disassembled and rebuilt, a relatively easy task since Korean houses are constructed without nails, in order to raise the area on which it stood by 70 centimeters so that it could be aligned with the level of the courtyard. Today, the *hanok* serves as a reception and meeting room. The thick ivy covering the walls of the original building behind represents a traditional visual expression of the seasons.

Above This interesting courtyard composition of old and new –
black brick wall, granite paving, and exposed concrete walls of
the Glass Forum – exemplifies Kim's architectural mix of Korea's
traditional spirit and modern culture. The red steel sculpture is
by Shin Ockjoo. Kim was especially fond of the carbonized clay
material called *jeondol*, which originated in China around 108 BC
during the Han Dynasty but was widely produced in Korea during
the Three Kingdoms period. Because of the material's superior
durability, *jeondol* was used for building tombs, towers, palace
floors and walls, fortresses, and temples. The black bricks used
in Kim's architecture, *jeonbyeokdol*, were later developed from
the ancient *jeondol* but are slightly smaller than the usual 19 x
9 x 7 centimeter size. "Because bricks must be laid by hand, one
by one, there are parallels with the endless process of human
maturing. The bricks are a readily available material and their
rough texture appeals to Korean sensibilities."

Opposite top left In the overall U-shaped ground plan of the Space
complex, the old tiled-roof *hanok* is sandwiched between the ivy-
covered original buildings and the modernist Glass Forum.

Opposite top right The granite cobblestone-paved foyer below the
reception area leads to the Space Theater, the venue for countless
performances and jazz concerts. Originally, there was a coffee shop
adjacent to the performance hall. The late architect and his friends
would fill the large glass jars lining its walls with coffee beans purchased on their worldwide travels at a time when coffee beans were
a rare commodity in Korea, and staff members were given coupons
to enjoy the precious brew alongside other customers. Below the
steps leading to the narrow alley in front of the building, Kim installed an old sculptural water basin from a temple.

Right A glass-enclosed bridge spanning the granite-paved courtyard connects the Glass Forum with the original buildings.

tribute to korean modernism

ARCHITECT **KIM SWOO-GEUN**

Above The composition of columns and grids crafted in Japanese *sugi* cedar wood is reminiscent of a Japanese temple. Iron fastenings crafted in a cross pattern are the only ornamentation on the wood construction. Buddhist architecture of the Nara period (AD 710–94) in Japan, built by Korean architects, is derivative of the Chinese Tang style. The overall emphasis was on structure imbued with frankness of construction and stable and balanced proportions, rather than on ornamentation.

Opposite A stunning wooden sculpture by Shim Moon-seup greets visitors as they proceed from the foyer to the living room, which is dominated by an exposed concrete grid ceiling, dramatically highlighted in the evenings by lights installed in the individual grids. Wassily chairs by Marcel Breuer in 1925 are grouped around a glass coffee table.

Located in Myeongryun-dong, an old residential area near the original site of Seoul National University, Korea's most prestigious university, this house was built in 1983 as a home-cum-atelier for an artist and his wife. With their four children grown up, the couple planned to work and retire here, and entrusted the job of designing the house to the wife's brother, the late Kim Swoo-geun (see page 175). Designed for his beloved sister when he was already bedridden, it turned out to be Kim's last project. Words from the maestro of contemporary Korean architecture are very much alive in the residence: "The essence of the human environment must be understood from an internal, spiritual point of view, not from a physical one." Although the second floor was partially renovated after the husband's death in 2002, the house remains largely as it was when it was first completed.

The three-story reinforced concrete above-ground structure and the fourth-level basement atelier have a combined floor area of 290 square meters. The façade is a monumental composition of columns and grids crafted in specially imported *sugi* – Japanese cedar wood. Modernist in design, with touches of Frank Lloyd Wright and Yoshimura Junzo (the architect's professor in Japan), it is also reminiscent of Japanese temples such as Toshodaiji in Nara in its display of simple and vital wooden components. The introduction of Buddhism to Japan from Korea in AD 538 was accompanied by a movement of people, including architects from the Korean kingdom of Baekje (18 BC–AD 660), whose art and architecture were characterized by elegance, refinement, and warmth. Along with influences and derivations from Chinese models, significant elements of Korean vernacular architecture were transmitted to Japan, as witnessed in the temples of Nara.

The grid motif continues into the interior spaces: the ceilings of the ground-floor living room and basement atelier are made of exposed concrete grids, while the doors and windows are of wooden latticework. The walls inside are largely finished in red brick, as is the floor in the entrance area. The living room floor is covered with 20-cm-wide oiled Douglas fir boards. Highlights of the house include the architect's signature spiral staircase topped with a skylight, which connects the four floors of the residence, and a wide band of papered latticed screens covering the south wall of the second floor. An analogy between glass windows and paper windows is often drawn in the discussion of Western versus Eastern aesthetics. Glass windows bring in light to reveal all physical presence, including slight imperfections, while paper windows filter light to obscure flaws, suffusing the room with a spiritual calmness. The traditional Korean house was built with deep eaves and papered windows, and thus its residents, furnishings, and domestic rituals were never revealed in direct light.

Marrying Korean elements with Western modernism, the residence is furnished with Korean antiques, modern art, contemporary furnishings, and understated flower arrangements. It exudes a nostalgic yet surprisingly modern ambience.

Left A signature feature of the architect's work, the spiral staircase occupies the west side of the house. Sensual plum red walls surround a graphic Bauhaus-inspired composition of graduated steel wedges supported by a single pole. The architect almost always topped his stairwells with a skylight and, in the case of this residence, added a window at the bottom for natural light to shine on the walls from below as well as above. On the brick wall, a large oil painting by Shin Ok-jin makes an interesting contrast to the low, narrow *gwae* chest below it.

Right The dining area is visible from the master bedroom, while the traditional study room and stairwell are located behind. The utilitarian dining table was specially designed by the architect for the owners. An extendable leaf is stored beneath the pinewood tabletop supported on two rolling cabinets, which hold daily clutter.

Below A study room or *sarangbang*, traditionally the master's space for intellectual pursuit and creative activity, referred to by the architect as the "Ultimate Space," was installed for the wife's use next to the dining area. The room is appointed with antique bookshelves lined with the Buddhist mantras she studies daily. Fresh flowers are offered each morning to the exquisite iron Buddha image sitting in the *sabangtakja* (see page 140, above).

Right and below The finest of craftsmanship is displayed in the *sugi* window system, which comprises three layers – storm shutters, framed glass windows, and papered latticed screens – which are slid open and shut along the multiple tracks built into the windowsill. Large pockets on the outside wall hold the storm windows when not in use. Cabinets faced with *sugi* doors, built beneath the windows, run the entire length of the room.

Above A low, late Joseon-period *gwae* chest is placed in front of a brick wall outside the master bedroom. A watercolor by the late architect hangs above. The antique wooden *gireogi* wild geese figure on the chest was used in the traditional marriage ceremony. Representing the newlyweds, the groom presented one to his mother-in-law, promising to maintain the virtues symbolized by the wild geese, such as keeping the same partner for life and not seeking a new partner if the other died. A simple flower arrangement in an old stone mortar is placed next to the geese. A wood-burning stove, a nostalgic addition, provides heat on days not cold enough to turn on the floor heating.

Below Another view of the signature spiral staircase shown on page 184.

Above Brick flooring and latticed glass extend into the foyer from the entrance. Here, guests remove their shoes before entering the house proper. The small garden outside is landscaped with a row of white birch trees whose foliage can be seen from the upstairs dining room. An old *dwiju* (see page 25, left), used for concealing everyday items, is the sole piece of furniture.

Below Another view of the *sarangbang* shown on page 185, below.

Right Latticework continues into the master bedroom where papered doors conceal a large wardrobe. A Scandinavian table purchased for its linear beauty, and resembling the traditional square *soban* tray table, stands before it. An understated flower arrangement provides an aesthetic touch.

reincarnation of a bygone era

ARCHITECT **CHOI WOOK**

Do Ga Hun, meaning "a beautiful house," opened to the public in 2004 as a café/restaurant and gallery for Korean art and crafts. The complex is composed of two meticulously restored buildings: a traditional *hanok* house built around 1900 and a Russian-style brick building ca. 1910. Located off a magnificent gingko-lined boulevard in Sagan-dong, across the road from the grand Joseon-period (1392–1910) Gyeongbokgung palace (see page 138), Do Ga Hun is tucked behind the imposing modern steel façade of Gallery Hyundai owned by the same family. Over the years, the family had observed the complex from their gallery window, but had never considered the possibility of acquiring it since it belonged to a Buddhist foundation. It was by sheer chance that the owner's son happened to discover on a realtor's website that the historical complex had suddenly been put up for sale. The buildings were bought the very next day.

Although no extant records specifically refer to these two buildings, scholars assume the *hanok* was built for a member of the royal family during the Joseon Dynasty because of its close proximity to the palace and its distinctive architectural details, reserved for the residences of royalty. These include decorative images (*jabsang*) on the roof and ornate engraving on the bronze joints of the narrow wooden ledge (*twoetmaru*) running along the front of the house. Planted with a beautiful 150-year-old gingko tree and large maple trees, the courtyard and the two historical buildings facing it were in a bad state of disrepair from years of neglect. Architect Choi Wook, who is engaged in similar renovation projects in the area, was commissioned to restore the buildings to their original glory, breathing new life into them.

Drawing on the expertise of traditional carpenters, Choi painstakingly restored the two buildings and, without compromising their integrity, added modern-day facilities for the restaurant and gallery. Although traditional carpenters are fast disappearing, some still live and work in this area where their forefathers built and restored palaces. Grime built up on the original woodwork of the *hanok* was fastidiously stripped by hand instead of by the easier sanding method that would have erased the delicate uneven surfaces of the timbers. The carpenters also crafted the latticed paper screens covering all the newly installed glass windows using traditional methods. However, the architect simplified the latticework in order to economize on costs. Says the architect, "I made a great effort to restore and preserve the original structures. The *hanok*, especially, was of such a beautiful and distinctive design that any additions had to be kept to an absolute minimum and be in keeping with the original building. I therefore made certain that my design was extremely discrete. All mechanical equipment is hidden from view except for the wine refrigerator." Since much of the two buildings as well as the original stone paving and brick boundary walls have been preserved, the architect added his own touches to existing details to create an evocative atmosphere for world-class dining and wining and the viewing of arts and crafts.

Opposite A view of the *hanok* from the back entrance of the complex shows its U-shaped layout and elegantly curved roof, called a *paljak* or *hapgak* roof. Among the various types of traditional roof, this is the most common on old buildings. It is also by far the most decorative and sumptuous of all styles with its four corners raised high and its triangular-shaped gables. In addition to the *giwa*-tiled roof, many original structures and details remain intact at Do Ga Hun, including the stone paving – covered here with autumn leaves shed by the gingko tree – brick wall, and wooden columns and beams.

Above Close-ups of the original stone paving and channels for water drainage reveal the craftsmanship and artistry of Korean artisans. By the time the current owner purchased the property, some of the courtyard pavers had been forced up by the roots of the old gingko tree. A small stone bridge, divided by a much wider waterway, connected the two buildings. The remains of the bridge have been converted to use as steps leading to the main entrance.

Left The low wooden ledge serves as a beautiful setting for displaying a collection of antique Haeju *soban* tables (see page 157, below) originating from northern regions of the Korean peninsula. It also provides a pleasant seating area in warmer weather. Joseon houses were often built with such intermediate ledges in the front and back of the house. Called *twoetmaru*, the narrow wooden ledge, sometimes fitted with low railings for safety, enabled people to walk from one room or area to another without having to put on or take off their shoes.

Below Fixed glass windows were installed throughout the café/restaurant to provide an open view of the beautiful courtyard and the building across from it. The sensuous outlines of the deep eaves, combined with the interplay of columns and beams inside, heighten the sensation of being inside a *hanok*. Although forced air heating is more common nowadays in commercial spaces, floor heating was selected in the restored *hanok* in an effort to protect the original woodwork from extreme dryness. An oak parquet floor with a distressed finish from Swedish manufacturer Pergo replaced the original flooring of the café/restaurant. A new wood deck was installed for alfresco dining. A basement, very unusual in traditional architecture, was discovered under the *hanok*'s right wing, and is now the wine cellar.

Top The graceful original arched entrance leads to the *hanok* on the left and the two-story Russian-style brick building on the right. The exterior of the brick building, just visible here beyond the gate, remains untouched. The interior, though, has been renovated as a gallery for a permanent collection of modern Korean masters as well as exhibitions of home furnishings and tableware, both traditional and contemporary. A third level was added to the building as a private room for entertaining clients.

Above The exquisite engraving seen on the bronze joints along the low wooden ledge of the *hanok* (see page 192) is evidence that the house was originally built for a family associated with the court.

Top Perched on roof corners and ridgelines to protect households from evil spirits and fire, figures were the preserve of palace buildings, monasteries and, in some rare cases, the homes of aristocrats. Called *jabsang*, the animal- or man-shaped clay figures were modeled after characters in the epic Chinese novel *Journey to the West*, written during the Ming Dynasty (AD 1368–1644).

Above A stone basin or *mulhwak* (see page 85, left), one of several designed by sculptor Lee Young-hak for the complex, catches rainwater from the copper gutter newly installed along the eaves of the roof.

Right The beautifully restored original columns and rafters display a five crossbeam structure, called *oryang*, which evolved from the more basic three crossbeam structure used in commoners' homes in the latter part of the Joseon period. An intricate system of mortise-and-tenon wooden joinery, capable of expanding according to changing temperatures and humidity, is used to assemble the magnificent interlocking roof frame, which is traditionally left exposed.

showcase of art

Having trained as an architect in the United States before returning home to oversee the family business, the owner of this palatial home, located in the older, more established, and hilly Gangbuk area of Seoul on the northern side of the Han River, has firm views on the subject of architecture and designed this residence as well as his former one. While many people prefer to live on the flatter landscape on the southern side of the river for its modern apartments and conveniences, this businessman, with a penchant for the finer things in life, chose to remain in the north to embrace its wondrous landscape and uninterrupted views.

He is surprisingly modest about the opulent 770-square meter home that sprawls over twelve split-levels. To preserve as much as possible of the expansive site's natural elements – a sharp drop to the southeast and groves of beautiful pine trees – the decision was made to design a three-story house on the sloping grounds closest to the street. It was only after the owner applied for building permits that he learned the area was governed by stringent building codes. "I regret the compromises made at the time, but people always say you have to build three homes to learn from your past mistakes. A transition of levels has always been an important spatial element for me, so the sloped site was ideal. As you see, I happen to like stairs, to the point that I installed more than were actually necessary. Architecturally speaking, they are interesting elements. Changes in level also allow spaces to have an autonomous identity."

One clearly sees what he means upon entering the house, as the living spaces are arranged in a multilevel layout joined by numerous steps and stairwells. Each room exudes a unique ambience with the use of different ceiling heights, window placements, and furnishings. Since completion in 1995, a south wing has been added, in 2001, to create more space for entertaining amidst an ever-expanding collection of contemporary art, modern furniture, and design objects.

Right Sunk below the level of the entrance foyer is the grand room, which soars to a height of well over six meters. Facing views to the southeast, with a large terrace wrapping its entire length, the room is dedicated to the works of contemporary Korean masters such as Lee Ufan, Ha Jong-hyun, Youn Myeung-ro, and Lim Choong-sup. Ample seating is provided by Philippe Starck couches designed for the famed New York Royalton Hotel. A sculpture in the image of a human hand by Lee Bul and another of a cigarette butt entitled "Fagend Study" by Claes Oldenburg grace the Fema-designed glass tables.

Left Another grand salon, this one in the new entertainment wing, is furnished with comfortable Alfa sofas and a high-gloss wenge-stained oak Rocco table, both designed by Emaf Progetti and manufactured by Zanotta, a Steinway grand piano, and a minibar. An early painting by Chung Yeon-hee on the exposed concrete wall forms a dramatic backdrop to a crescent-shaped wood sculpture by Lim Choong-sup and a large porcelain vessel by Yang Gu, modeled on the *dal hang-ari* style – the epitome of eighteenth-century Joseon aesthetics representing the pride of the people as well as the rediscovery of the individual self. Because of its size, the two halves were hand molded separately and then joined – as in the past. Originally, they were used for storing condiments in the kitchens of aristocrats.

Above Truly an audiophile's dream, the audio room is equipped with a top-of-the-line McIntosh power amplifier system, Roksan turntable, JBL speakers, Maxell reel tape recorder, and an amazing collection of records. The system pipes music to speakers throughout the residence, including water-proof speakers on the terrace and in various entertainment spots dispersed throughout the large garden. Having meticulously designed the shelves in 1995 to fit the dimensions of his equipment, the owner ruefully admits that he did not forsee the coming of plasma TV, so the Sony tube TV remains a permanent fixture. To compensate, a ceiling projector and screen roll down in front of the shelves for large-screen viewing. Classic design pieces – Barcelona chairs by Mies van der Rohe and a glass coffee table by Isamu Noguchi – as well as a sculpture by Ben Vautier (not shown), a spur of the moment purchase made in Saint Paul de Vence after lunching at the famed La Colombe d'Or, fill the rest of the room.

Right Multiple stairways divide the residence's large volume into separate spaces, each stamped with a distinctive personality. They also serve to showcase works on paper by leading twentieth-century artists. An elegant nineteenth-century pinewood *bandaji chaekjang* book chest with inverted ends is a striking item on the landing.

Opposite above The Eames lounge chair, ottoman, and walnut stool placed next to the large windows on the opposite side of the salon shown on page 198, provide for leisurely gazing at the water feature and outdoor art: Seo Jungguk's metal bamboo sculpture and Zaha Hadid's aerodynamic aluminum bench.

Opposite below Facing the window in the mezzanine atrium, which also serves as a study for the busy entrepreneur, is a Quaderna writing table designed by Super Studio in plastic laminate silk-screened with black grid work, and manufactured by Zanotta. The popular Tolomeo lamp designed by Michele de Lucci sits on the writing table, while a polycarbonate Bourgie lamp by Philippe Starck sits on the side table flanked by a pair of Wassily armchairs. On the wall hangs a Bang & Olufsen stereo system and aluminum CD cabinet by Shigeru Uchida. Miniatures of the 1960s award-winning Panton chair occupy the windowsill.

Above Every room in the residence is furnished with design classics from the owner's extensive collection of museum-quality furniture. Here, in the mezzanine atrium overlooking the grand room, is the Mies van der Rohe day bed. A painting by Alexander Calder hangs above, while Roy Lichtenstein's teacup series lines the ledge. Art magazines and catalogues are neatly stored in acrylic cubes designed by artist Yang Juhae (see page 89) with her signature bar code motifs. Suspended from the ceiling of the adjacent void is a stunning mechanical sculpture by Choi U-ram.

Top Reflections of the pine trees in the garden water feature produce a beautiful still-life image.

Above Although the owner concentrates on collecting contemporary art and modern design, he nonetheless reserves one room in the house for Korean antiques. A few pieces here are from his late mother's collection, such as the late Joseon-period *soban* tray table on which a fine example of a Goryeo period (AD 918–1392) celadon tea bowl is placed.

Top Antique boxes, including this one, formerly used by aristocrat scholars to store letters and documents are displayed on the bookshelf in the "Korean room."

Above Of superb proportions and simple dignity, a stone pagoda from the Silla period (575 BC–AD 935) stands in front of the natural pine tree grove in the eastern corner of the vast grounds. Pagodas were believed to balance or mend "wounds" in the earth, unlucky spots recognized by geomancers. Ancient records show that Korean pagodas were originally made of wood, earth, and bricks.

Above A pair of *mungwanseok* stone guardians (see pages 158–9) stand in a shaded garden inside the entrance gate. The architectural form of the exposed concrete façade traces the lines of the curved site and is echoed by the elegant stone pathway meandering through the garden. Indigenous Korean plants such as the large maple tree, wild orchids, azaleas, and bamboo are planted alongside.

Right White petunia blossoms offset a rare piece from an early to mid-Joseon period tombstone intricately carved with dragon and flower motifs.

masterpiece of confucian architecture

Nestled in the isolated village of Pungsan in the Andong area, Byeongsan Seowon was originally built in the mid-Goryeo Dynasty (AD 918–1392) as a school for the aristocrat Yu family. It was relocated in 1572 to its present site by Yu Seong-ryong, distinguished family member, eminent scholar-official, and foreign minister during the reign of King Seonjo (1552–1608). Destroyed during the Japanese invasion of 1592, Byeongsan Seowon was rebuilt after Yu's death in 1607, but was not officially recognized as a Confucian *seowon* (academy) until 1613 when a shrine was built on the grounds to commemorate the respected *seonbi* (teacher and philosopher). Embracing the ideal of a mind in complete harmony with nature, which became deeply rooted in Korean philosophy during the Joseon period, Byeongsan Seowon is a masterpiece of Neo-Confucian architecture representing the uniqueness of Korea's architectural heritage. It was among the forty-seven *seowon* surviving a nationwide closure of academies in 1868 to correct the disproportionate economic and social power that the academies had acquired. Although stone was abundant and widely used in the construction of buildings, Byeongsan Seowon was built entirely in wood except for its foundations. The intrinsic beauty of wood is highlighted by the integrity of ancient engineering that employed skilled wood joinery, which also facilitated its relocation.

The exquisite setting of the *seowon*, facing Byeong Mountain and the Nakdong River flowing at its base, sets this academy apart from others and deeply informs its architecture. Although the buildings maintain the typical square layout and building–garden relationship of a Confucian academy, all parts, including the boundary walls, have been carefully designed to not obstruct views or disrupt the natural landscape. The main buildings in the compound include Ipgyodang auditorium on the north side, Mandaeru pavilion on the south side, two student dormitories, Dongjae and Seojae, on the east and west sides, and Jeondeoksa shrine. The most impressive building is Mandaeru pavilion, which is raised above the others to fully communicate with the beauty of the surrounding landscape. Steps hewn from a single log lead up to a breathtaking view from the wide-open pavilion. The pavilion inspires a profound appreciation of "nothingness" and of Confucian aesthetics: eliminating the inessential and seeking beauty in humble, unadorned things.

In the academy, young Yu family members were taught the concepts of *taegeuk* (the Great Ultimate) and *li* and *gi* (best defined as the "primal force of the universe" creating natural phenomena) in order to achieve internal harmony. The scholar-officials of the *yangban* class made up the Korean élite. Intense study of Confucian texts and the practice of calligraphy were required to pass difficult examinations for government service. "Korean scholars," points out University of California Berkeley Museum curator James Steward, "considered themselves, like their Chinese counterparts, first and foremost men of letters imbued with what was often described as the 'fragrance of writing' and the 'spirit of books'."

Previous page and above The unassuming beauty of Mandaeru pavilion derives from its rustic unhewn pinewood roof rafters and the integrity of ancient building techniques. True to the pavilion typology, there are no walls or doors in the pavilion. The columns are round so as not to detract from the intense interaction with the natural landscape. Steps hewn from a single log lead up to the wide-open floor. Slightly curved logs support the floor to express harmony with nature, while straight logs support the roof to create visual stability. Devoid of ornamentation, apart from the railings, or visually obtrusive elements, the architecture signifies an "emptying of the mind." Frugality and austerity, guiding principles of Confucian thought, define the space where students were expected to purify their minds and concentrate on their studies.

Right The pavilion viewed from Seojae dormitory. The natural beauty of the wooden materials, sequence of round columns, and black *giwa* roof tiles harmonize with the framed view of Byeong Mountain beyond.

Above Stone column foundations, as seen here under Mandaeru pavilion, were mostly sculpted in relatively even sizes and shapes but never honed to a smooth surface, thus requiring the bottom end of wooden columns to be "molded" to the uneven surfaces on the top of the blocks before being erected. This was accomplished by hanging the columns on a rope above the stones and using a *graeng-i* knife – a unique Korean invention in bamboo resembling a large H-shaped pincette – to shave the wood to fit the granite surface snugly. Columns stand completely stable without the use of fixatives.

Right Traditional architects devised special techniques to create visual stability as well as elegance of form. The corner columns were extended slightly higher in relation to the other columns to create delicate eave lines, enabling massive roofs to acquire an elegant shape. The deep eaves provided ample shade, necessary in the hot summer months. Both in design and engineering, artificial contrivances were eschewed, allowing the natural beauty of the materials and techniques employed to be highlighted.

Left The garden, landscaped with crepe myrtle trees, is seen at the rear of Ipgyodang auditorium.

Above Pavilions, such as Mandaeru shown here, were erected as a focal point of every academy, usually near the main entrance. They formed an ideal stage for group debates as well as individual spiritual encounters with nature.

Right Viewed from Mandaeru pavilion, Ipgyodang auditorium consists of the central lecture hall and two quarters on either side for resident scholars. The original plaque bearing its name hangs under the eaves. The smaller buildings facing the courtyard on the east and west sides are the student dormitories Dongjae and Seojae, which both have similar constructions: an open wooden floor area flanked by two floor-heated rooms. Traditionally, rooms were small and sparsely furnished, but were easily rearranged with partition doors. A lack of inner space was compensated for by the latticed windows, designed to be raised, which faced the outer courtyards, thereby opening up the interior to the outdoors.

Above Byeong Mountain, partially shrouded in misty clouds, forms a spectacular backdrop to the elegant curved-roof Mandaeru pavilion viewed from Ipgyodang auditorium. The first consideration in choosing a site for a *seowon* was the beauty of its surroundings. Only a site endowed with divine spiritual energy was believed capable of producing fine noblemen. Removed from secular life, the scholars were expected to reach spiritual enlightenment, recognizing the importance of moral ethics and becoming one with nature. *Mugunghwa* (Rose of Sharon) trees seen in the courtyard are designated as Korea's national flower since the name means perseverance and determination.

Top Dongjae, the east dormitory, and the roof of Mandaeru pavilion are seen through the opened back doors of Ipgyodang auditorium. As with the dormitories, external fireplaces were built into the stone embankments to provide *ondol* heating (see page 138). Smoke from the wood fed into the external fireplace circulated under the floor before exiting from the flues seen beneath the floor.

Above The sequence of steps leading up to the academy compound is seen through Bongnyemun gate.

square within a square

ARCHITECT **CHO BYOUNGSOO**

Above The entrance to the industrial-looking concrete box is composed of two sets of doors: a sliding steel door on the outside and a pinewood door on the inside. Whenever the house is occupied, the sliding steel door is fully opened to reveal a covered entrance area with a small open courtyard, as seen on page 222, above right.

Opposite The open courtyard in the center of the house – the "square within a square" – fondly referred to as the "moon viewing court" by the architect, glows beneath the star-studded sky.

Overlooking brilliant green rice fields and backed by a small hill, this modest yet refined exposed concrete box in Sugok-ri, about 60 kilometers from Seoul, was designed by architect Cho Byoungsoo for himself and his family. It was conceived as a place for working, entertaining, and tending a small vineyard with hopes of eventually producing an annual yield of a hundred bottles. Constrained by a limited legal building area, the architect originally drew up plans for a two-story house, only to realize that the height of the building would obstruct views of the tree-clad hill behind. Faced with the challenge of opening up a single-story house to nature, his imaginative response was to close off the house instead and engage in a concentrated dialogue with nature from within. The result is an austere, industrial-looking square block pierced by small openings, which looks inward to a central open-air courtyard pool. In contrast to the surrounding rice fields and sloped terrain backed with natural forests, the introverted house is bold, graphic, and disciplined. Over time, grass, wild flowers, and grapevines will take full root and nature will begin to transform the building, asserting itself over the man-made structure.

The few openings perforating the walls of the box-shaped structure are devoid of frames or glass. They are simply covered with sliding steel doors set on rails, and hinged steel shutters to reinforce the industrial look. The openings are securely closed on the inside by wooden doors and shutters. A flat roof slab forms a neat top to the box. Various methods for casting the concrete roof were discussed with the contractor before the architect decided that an old handcrafted technique was the perfect solution. Successive layers of concrete were poured for the roof, each diligently leveled by a trowel, forcing excess water or air to rise to the surface. The result was a flat concrete slab 20 cm thick, completely crack free and impervious to water. Ten massive wooden columns that the architect had purchased for future use, placed five meters apart in an alternating zigzag pattern, provide the sole support for the roof.

An intense dialogue with nature is initiated by the 7.5 by 7.5-meter void carved into the center of the building. A shallow reflecting pool filled with wild grass and boulders, excavated on site, occupies almost the entire open square. A neatly cropped view of the sky, a hallmark of the architect's work, appears above it. The courtyard is an extension of the interior space. Two sets of folding glass doors open fully to bring in light, wind, the seasonal colors of the pond, and the soothing sounds of cicadas and crickets. The level of the floor in the glassed-in minimalist house is carried through to the outside, providing continuity and visually expanding the space. The alternate alignment of the wooden columns placed both in and out of the courtyard further reinforces the spatial unity.

Inside the house, the palette shifts to warm and natural materials – bamboo veneer flooring and pinewood ceilings and doors – juxtaposed with exposed concrete. The overall ambience is minimalist, but at the same time exudes a rustic barn-like feeling, probably due to the fact that the owner is a part-time resident of Montana. The raw interior finishes provide a perfect backdrop for the massive wooden columns, Korean antiques, and a collection of salvaged architectural materials that resemble primitive art.

Left The architect's desk, made of Douglas fir wood, is placed in front of the southern opening. Pinewood doors reminiscent of barn doors, and shutters hinged on wall hooks as in vernacular architecture (see page 142), are fully opened to reveal neatly cropped views of the natural surroundings. Steel shutters, designed to be propped open on diagonally cut steel rods, close off the opening near the floor from the outside. An imposing *dwiju* grain chest from the late Joseon period (1392–1910) – its large size due to the fact that it was used for storing sacks of grain, not loose grain – stores books and magazines.

Above left and right The simple layout of the house wraps around the square pool. Uninterrupted floor-to-ceiling glass walls enclose two sides of the courtyard while folding glass doors open on the other two sides to allow a natural flow of air. Sharing space in the simple pond with a variety of water grasses and water lilies are two large boulders found on site, their crevices planted with delicate patches of moss and wild flowers.

Left All openings perforating the walls of the box-shaped structure are devoid of frames or glass. The large opening on the south wall, as shown from the inside above, is covered with sliding steel doors set on rails, and securely closed on the inside by wooden doors.

Right Four rows of grape vines have been planted along gray-painted steel and wire supports designed to harmonize with the industrial look of the house. Three massive granite slabs, each weighing 8–10 tons, were transported from Iksan in South Jolla Province. They provide a dramatic setting on which to enjoy a game of *baduk* (Korean chess), a glass of wine at sunset, or simply a view of the starry night sky.

Above A view of the hallway leading from the open-plan kitchen to the entrance area. The pinewood ceiling and shutters exude a pleasant woody aroma. The "gallery," as shown on page 221, above, is seen across the courtyard.

Opposite Ceramic pieces by a Japanese artist add interest to a corner of the cast-concrete kitchen counter adjacent to the living area. Brushed aluminum cabinetry surrounds the Samsung refrigerator. The pair of rustic benches, purchased from a local carpenter who makes furniture when he stumbles across inspiring pieces of wood, provides seating for casual dining in colder seasons. Alfresco dining is the norm in warmer weather. The sink vanity counter between the bathroom and bedroom is visible in the background. Although the counter is in the subterranean area on the east side of the house, it receives plenty of light from the frameless skylight above, composed of a thick glass panel made from seven sheets of glass set directly into the concrete roof.

Right A cast-concrete fireplace divides the architect's work area and the living room. Two sets of folding glass doors open fully to bring in light, wind, and the seasonal colors of the pond. The level of the floor in the glassed-in minimalist house is carried through to the outside, providing continuity and visually expanding the space. The alternate alignment of the wooden columns placed both in and out of the courtyard further reinforces the spatial unity. The entire floor of the house is *ondol* heated. The single bedroom (not shown) is located in the east side of the house that is sunk into the sloped terrain. The dark, windowless room, a stark contrast to the brightness of the rest of the house, is cosy and conducive to sound sleep. Typical of a casual country lifestyle, the living room areas do double duty as impromptu bedrooms with traditional bedding laid out, accommodating any number of guests.

Above The concrete fireplace surrounds are cast with an indent for storing logs, a thoughtful detail found in many of the architect's works (see pages 80–1). An oil painting by Han Man Young housed in a mirrored cube sits on one of the speakers.

Left A close-up of the pinewood doors converted into hinged shutters near the architect's desk (see page 214).

Above left A long steel bench covered with a pinewood seat was specially designed for reflection: gazing at the ever-changing colors and reflections of the pond and at the moon through the open roof. An old rusted anvil reclaimed from a blacksmith's shop makes a sculptural statement at the far end of the bench.

Left An old scholar's brush box, which now holds drawing utensils, sits at one end of the architect's desk (see page 214, above).

Above The hallway leading from the entrance area to the architect's desk serves as a gallery. An aesthetic composition of reclaimed columns and old doors propped against the wall forms an "exhibition" of primitive art.

Above At the end of a sloped driveway, a quirky pagoda made of rusted iron soup kettles called *sot* sits in front of a retaining wall constructed of boulders excavated on site.

Above right The covered entrance area has a small open courtyard. Here, bamboo trees soar above the building through the open roof, and in a play of light and shadow cast exquisite shadows on the exposed concrete wall. A small stone figure, composed of a primitive human figure and a found head-shaped rock, "guards" the house from within the bamboo grove. An old Korean pinewood pillar has been carved out to make a convenient seat for removing shoes before entering the house.

Right Water lilies thrive in an old stone trough, originally used for animal feed, in the entrance courtyard.

Opposite A solitary opening punctures the south wall of the building. A set of pinewood doors encloses it on the inside while a gray-painted sliding steel door encloses it on the outside. A Corten steel canopy above has been deliberately left untreated to develop a patina of rust. The geometric composition of the three materials forms a striking image against the exposed concrete wall.

Credits

Arumjigi Culture Keepers Foundation
3 Anguk-dong, Jongno-gu
Seoul 110-240, Korea
Tel: +82 2 741 8373
E-mail: webmaster@arumjigi.org
http://www.arumjigi.org

Cho Byoungsoo
Cho Byoungsoo Architects
Bozeman Office:
401 W. Dickerson Street
Bozeman, MT 59715, USA
Tel: +1 406 582 7481
E-mail: byoungcho2003@hotmail.com
Seoul Office:
3rd Floor Sil Building
55-7 Banpo 4-dong, Seocho-gu
Seoul 137-803, Korea
Tel: +82 2 537 8261

Choi Du Nam
Choi Du Nam Architects
#1501 Garden Tower Building
98-78 Unni-dong, Jongno-gu
Seoul 110-795, Korea
Tel: +82 2 766 4585
E-mail: dcaa@chol.com

Choi Wook
One O One
ML Building
126-2 Susong-dong, Jongno-gu
Seoul 110-140, Korea
Tel: +82 2 739 6363
E-mail: studio101@empal.com
http://www.oneoonedesign.com

Do Ga Hun Art & Wine
109 Sagan-dong, Jongno-gu
Seoul 110-190, Korea
Tel: +82 2 3210 2100
http://www.dogahun.com

Kim Choon
Hexa Design and Consulting
208-18 Buam-dong, Jongno-gu
Seoul 110-817, Korea
Tel: +82 2 396 0445
E-mail: kim@hdnc.net

Kim In Cheurl
Archium Architects
118-10 Yongdap-dong, Seongdong-gu
Seoul 133-849, Korea
Tel: +82 2 2214 9852
E-mail: archium@chol.net
http://www.archium.co.kr

Kim Kai Chun
Professor, Department of Interior
  Design
College of Design
Kookmin University
861-1 Jeongneung-dong, Seongbuk-gu
Seoul 136-702, Korea
Tel: +82 2 910 4440
E-mail: kck@kookmin.ac.kr

Kim Youngseok Jeontong Hanbok
56 Sogyeok-dong, Jongno-gu
Seoul 110-200, Korea
Tel: +82 2 725 1257

Lee Chonghwan
Omni Design
2nd Floor, 148-9 Samseong-dong,
Gangnam-gu
Seoul 135-090, Korea
Tel: +82 2 538 8224
E-mail: belllee@omnidesign.co.kr
http://www.omnidesign.co.kr

Lock Museum
187-8 Dongsung-dong, Jongno-gu
Seoul 110-810, Korea
Tel: +82 2 766 6494
E-mail: choiga123@hanmail.net
http://www.lockmuseum.org

Michael McNeil & Chung Jaewoong
K+C Design LLC
41 West 57th Street, 2nd Floor
New York, NY 10019, USA
Tel: +1 212 716 1300
E-mail: mvmcneil@kcdesignllc.com

Minn Sohn Joo
Associate Professor
Department of Architectural and Urban
  Engineering
Yonsei University

134 Shinchon-dong, Seodaemun-gu
Seoul 120-749, Korea
Tel: + 82 2 2123 5781
E-mail: msj@yonsei.ac.kr

Seung H-Sang
Iroje Architects & Planners
2-8 Dongsung-dong, Jongno-gu
Seoul 110-809, Korea
Tel: + 82 2 763 2010
E-mail: hseung@iroje.com
http://www.iroje.com

Space Group
219 Wonseo-dong, Jongno-gu
Seoul 110-280, Korea
Tel: +82 2 763 0771
E-mail: master@spacea.com
http://www.spaceA.com

Han van der Stap
Han Design Concept
Yong-hwa Building, 3rd Floor
654-14 Shinsa-dong, Gangnam-gu
Seoul 135-897, Korea
Tel: +82 2 512 9766
Email: archi@handesign.co.kr
http://www.handesign.co.kr

Jean-Michel Wilmotte
Wilmotte and Associates
68, rue du Faubourg Saint-Antoine
75012 Paris, France
Tel: +33 1 5302 2222
E-mail: wilmotte@wilmotte.fr
http:// www.wilmotte.fr

We would like to thank Ryu Seok Ran, Oh Sun Young, and Seo Gil Sung for their hard work at the photo shoots, and Noor Azlina Yunus for her expert editing. Special thanks are also due to Alice J. Choy, Woo Chang Hwan of Yea Rang Bang, and Jung Jaeho for their references and advise. Lastly, we would like to express our deep gratitude to the home owners and their families, business owners, architects, and designers who extended their hospitality and co-operation during the preparation of this book.